Introduction to
AutoCAD
2005

J.T. Roberts, B.Sc., M.Sc.

PAYNE-GALLWAY
PUBLISHERS LTD

Published by Payne-Gallway Publishers Limited
Payne-Gallway is an imprint of Harcourt Education Ltd
Halley Court, Jordan Hill, Oxford, OX2 8EJ

Tel: 01865 888070 Fax: 01865 314029
E-mail: orders@payne-gallway.co.uk Web: www.payne-gallway.co.uk

© J.T. Roberts 2005
First edition published 2005

10 09 08 07 06 05
10 9 8 7 6 5 4 3 2 1

British Library Cataloguing in Publication Data is available from the British Library on request

ISBN 1 904467 86 5

Copyright notice

Cover design © Richard Chasemore
Design & Artwork by Direction Advertising & Design Ltd
Printed in Malta by Gutenberg Press

AutoCAD is a registered trademark of Autodesk, Inc., in the USA and/or other countries.

Ordering Information
You can order from:

Payne-Gallway, FREEPOST (OF1771),
PO Box 381, Oxford OX2 8BR
Tel: 01865 888070
Fax: 01865 314029
E-mail: orders@payne-gallway.co.uk
Web: www.payne-gallway.co.uk

001.644 3 A

The cover drawings were prepared by the author using AutoCAD 2005 and rendered with 3D Studio Max to
show the possibilities. The rendered cover drawings from this book and from *Introduction to AutoCAD 2002*
are available on the publisher's website, as is the completed MGM Electronics drawing.

3D unrendered blocks are available for use with the office drawing from the publisher's website. These
blocks include indoor objects such as furniture, shelving and people, and outdoor objects such as trees,
vehicles and resting furniture.

Acknowledgements

I would like to thank the talented Jonathan Dean Morgan for his 3D Studio interpretation of my ideas on the
front cover of this book. I would also like to express my gratitude to my good friend Ray Pugsley for taking
on the onerous task of correcting my mistakes and omissions. Special thanks to the meticulous Matthew
Strawbridge and Olwen Turchetta of Harcourt Education for making this a better book.

For my wife, Monica,
one of the gifted people.

Contents

Preface

This book is an update of the popular *Introduction to AutoCAD 2002* and includes as many of the new AutoCAD 2004 and AutoCAD 2005 commands as time and space would allow.

No knowledge is assumed prior to this course of study. However, keyboard competence would be an advantage.

The Intended Audience

This book may be used as an introduction for

> *Level 2 City & Guilds Certificate in Computer-Aided Design, Course No. 4353-02;*
> *Level 3 City & Guilds Certificate in Computer-Aided Design, Course No. 4353-03.*

It can be used also to introduce Further and Higher Education students on Built Environment and Engineering courses to the concepts of using AutoCAD in a professional manner.

Last, but not least, the book will be very useful for those of you practising design of any flavour and will enable you to tackle complex projects quickly.

Earlier and Different Versions of AutoCAD

This book can also be used with AutoCAD 2000 without undue confusion. I have used it with AutoCAD LT 2000 and upwards. The newer AutoCAD 2004 and 2005 commands are highlighted using icons at the side of the page, so can be easily skipped over if you are using an earlier version of the software.

Practice Drawing Exercises

In response to feedback, I have included a number of basic 'mechanical' type practice drawings which could be attempted before tackling the book. Exercises in drawing with coordinates and object snaps are also included.

I have estimated the completion time of this book to be approximately 20–30 hours (excluding the drawing exercises).

The methods described in this book are not meant to be prescriptive or definitive. They are the way in which I approached the problems. Any suggestions for improvements would be gratefully accepted. Please contact me by e-mail at jeffroberts@72fernlea.freeserve.co.uk

Jeff Roberts

Introduction

What is AutoCAD?

AutoCAD is a draughting and design software package. It was first sold in 1982 under the name MicroCAD and ran under the CP/M operating system. Since those early days, AutoCAD has undergone many improvements and changes, and today it has been translated into 18 languages and is used by millions of people worldwide.

Who is AutoCAD for?

Quite simply, if anything needs to be drawn then AutoCAD can be used to do it. Apart from an artist's sketching (and even here the boundaries are becoming more and more blurred with each release of AutoCAD) there is very little for which AutoCAD cannot be used. Architectural drawings, mechanical assemblies, transportation, retail space modelling, aeronautical and marine design, cartography, assembly line production diagrams and residential design are but a few examples where AutoCAD is used extensively. In addition, the availability of a plethora of third-party software packages which 'bolt-on' and work from within AutoCAD make it the designer's dream.

What if I Use an Earlier Version of AutoCAD?

If you use AutoCAD R13, or an earlier version, then this book will help you to update your skills very quickly by showing the 'icon' short-cuts. The new wording that AutoCAD 2005 uses in its command-line sequences is used throughout the book; if you use AutoCAD R14 then this will get you up to speed quickly.

I've Never Drawn in 3D!

Even if you have never drawn in 3D, used Model Space and Paper Space or created a new User Coordinate System (UCS), you will find that the book introduces these using easy-to-follow instructions.

Many existing users of AutoCAD are confused by Paper Space and moving the UCS icon to a new drawing plane. The book approaches these topics on a step-by-step basis so that you can gain the necessary skills and confidence as you progress.

What's in the Book?

The book approaches the problem of learning AutoCAD 2005 from a new angle – a scenario is developed in the form of a fictitious building, starting from a blank electronic drawing sheet and ending with a 3D building. The final drawing shows three different views placed on a border with drawing titling, etc. This method was chosen to simulate, as closely as possible, how the drawing would be approached in a live situation. At the end of this book you should have gained the skills and confidence to attempt quite complex drawings.

In addition, drawing exercises which are not connected with the scenario have been included. Basic drawing techniques, such as the different methods of coordinate input, may be practised using the exercises before attempting the book.

Fast Track

WWW   If you have some knowledge of AutoCAD and want to update certain skills without spending time going through the whole of the book, you can download the drawing, from the publisher's website, in the correct state for the beginning of the chapter you want to start working on.

The Scenario

The scenario drawing is the fictitious administrative headquarters of a small electronics company. The drawing is developed from a blank screen – in much the same way that you would start any drawing. The drawing is carried out in 2D, with walls, doors and windows being constructed for the internal detail, and landscaping features such as a paved patio, pond, driveway and boundary wall added externally.

Reusable symbols are created in the form of the furniture. The drawing is dimensioned and textual data added as annotations. Finally, the drawing is converted from 2D to 3D and a tiled, pitched roof is added. Three views of the drawing are created on a drawing border, the drawing title details are added and, lastly, the drawing is plotted.

Icons at the Side of the Page

Text in a **Bold** style (e.g. **DRAW/Line**) signifies an AutoCAD command or dialogue box text to be accessed through the keyboard, screen icons or pull-down menus. Icons used at the side of the page indicate that the command can be accessed through that button.

The 2005 symbol indicates that the feature is new to AutoCAD 2005 or is one that has been updated and changed.

The 2004 symbol indicates that the feature is new to AutoCAD 2004 or is one that has been updated and changed and is still available in AutoCAD 2005.

The Tip symbol gives extra information to help you complete a function more efficiently or in a different manner.

The Note symbol alerts you to additional information which could be helpful.

WWW   This symbol indicates files which are on the publisher's website and are available for download.

Chapter 1 – The Basics

Launching AutoCAD

To launch AutoCAD

- Double-click the AutoCAD 2005 icon on your Windows desktop or click on **Start**, **Programs**, **Autodesk**, **AutoCAD 2005** and **the AutoCAD 2005** program, as shown in Figure 1.1.

Your Windows setup may be different but you should have a similar layout to that shown in Figure 1.1.

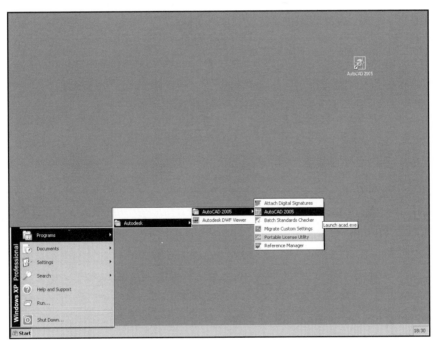

Figure 1.1. Windows screen showing AutoCAD 2005 menu item and icon

Once you have activated AutoCAD the **Startup** dialogue box appears, as shown in Figure 1.2.

- Click the **Start from Scratch** button, indicated in Figure 1.2. Click **OK**.

This will present you with the drawing screen and editor, as shown in Figure 1.3. Your screen should look similar to Figure 1.3 but you may have more or different toolbars visible. When we start the target drawing we will use the **Wizards** option to set up the drawing unit type and drawing area size.

1

Start from Scratch button

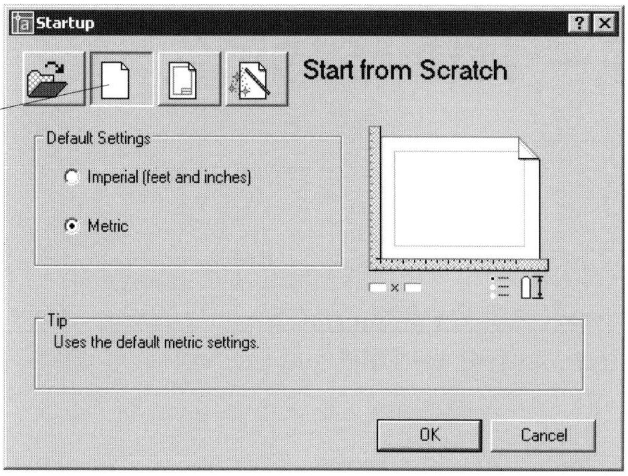

Figure 1.2. *AutoCAD 2005 Startup dialogue box*

*If you don't see the **Startup** dialogue box it means that the option to start a drawing with the dialogue box is turned off. You can turn this on with **TOOLS/Options**. Click on the **System** tab and on the right hand side of the box you will see the **Startup** drop-down menu. Change this to **Show Startup dialog box** and click on **OK**. Exit AutoCAD and start again. AutoCAD will then display the **Startup** dialogue box, as shown in Figure 1.2.*

*Experienced users should note that the **AutoCAD Today** dialogue box found in earlier versions of AutoCAD is no longer available.*

*Throughout this book the background screen colour to the drawing is white for clarity of printing. Your drawing, however, will probably have a background colour of black. To change this use **TOOLS/Options**. Click on the **Display** tab and then the **Colors** button. The **Color Options** dialogue box will appear. Under **Window Element** select **Model tab background**. In the **Color** drop-down menu select a suitable colour and click on **Apply and Close**. The **Color Options** dialogue box will disappear. Click on **OK** in the **Options** dialogue box. Whatever colour background you use, only the objects are printed; the background colour is for display purposes only.*

Figure 1.3 shows the screen which will appear after you have clicked on the 'Start from Scratch' button.

Figure 1.4 shows a customised screen with two floating toolbars and one docked toolbar loaded. The methods for loading, docking and moving toolbars are covered in Chapter 4.

Figures 1.3 and 1.4 show alternative ways of displaying the **UCS** icon.

Use of the tool palettes shown in Figure 1.4 is covered in Chapter 6.

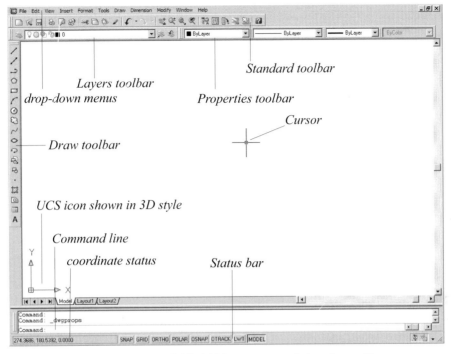

Figure 1.3. AutoCAD 2005 screen and drawing editor

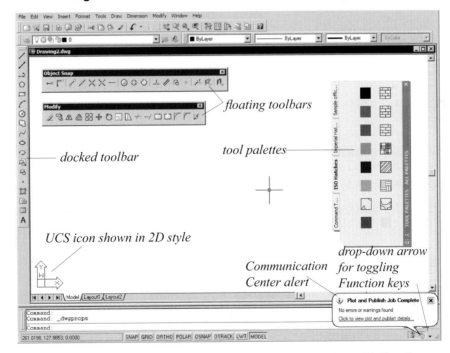

Figure 1.4. AutoCAD 2005 screen and drawing editor with floating toolbars, tool palettes and Communication Center active

The Keyboard

AutoCAD has special uses for certain parts of the keyboard. The keys prefixed with the letter 'F' (F1–F12) are called **function keys** and their uses are listed below. Some of the buttons on the **Status bar** (see Figure 1.3) are identical in operation to the function keys.

F1   AutoCAD help

F2   Toggle between graphics window and command window

F3   Object Snap mode on/off

F5   Cycle through isometric planes

F6   Coordinate display on/off

F7   Grid mode on/off

F8   Orthographic mode on/off

F9   Snap mode on/off

F10   Polar mode on/off

F11   Object Tracking mode on/off

The other keys that have special uses are:

Esc   Cancels the last operation

Spacebar Acts as the **Enter** key when in Drawing mode (inserts a space in Text mode)

<   Used when specifying polar coordinates: any figure following the < is an angle

@   Used when specifying relative and polar coordinates, and translates as 'in relation to the last position of the cursor'

Enter   Completes an operation

Ctrl+0   The **Control** and **Zero** keys, when pressed simultaneously, close all toolbars, allowing more space to draw. Repeat **Ctrl+0** to reinstate the toolbars.

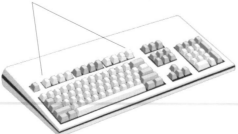

Function or 'F' keys, 1–12

Figure 1.5. The keyboard

4

The Pointing Device

Pointing can be done either with a mouse or a digitising tablet: AutoCAD can be set up to accept both methods.

The mouse can be either a two- or three-button model. Normally the left button is the 'Pick' or select button. The right button is the equivalent of **Enter** on the keyboard and completes a command sequence. It also reactivates the last command after a command sequence is completed. The right button can also be programmed via the **User Preferences** tab on the **TOOLS/Options** menu. The middle button on a three-button mouse can be programmed for almost any AutoCAD function, but that is outside the scope of this book.

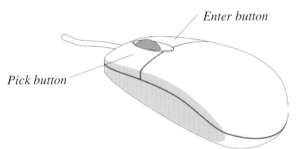

Enter button

Pick button

Figure 1.6. *The mouse*

*To customise the right mouse button use **TOOLS/Options**. The **Options** dialogue box appears. Click on the **User Preferences** tab and under the **Windows Standard Behavior** rectangle place a check mark in **Shortcut menus in drawing area**. This will activate the **Right-Click Customization** button. Click this button and the **Right-Click Customization** dialogue box will appear, as shown in Figure 1.7.*

*If you want the right-click to replicate the **Enter** key on the keyboard, click on the **Enter** radio button in the **Command Mode** rectangle to make it active.*

*To enable the time-sensitive right-click, place a check in the **Turn on time-sensitive right-click** dialogue box and change the **milliseconds** value to suit yourself. You may need to experiment with the timings.*

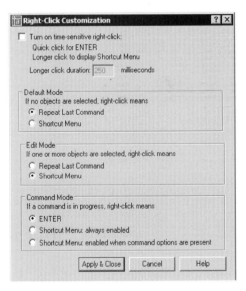

Figure 1.7. *The Right-Click Customization dialogue*

*Select the options you want, then click on **Apply and Close.** Click on **OK** when the **Options** dialogue box reappears.*

Similarly, digitising tablet puck buttons can be programmed for almost any function. In both cases only the 'pick' button cannot be reallocated.

Figure 1.8 shows the digitising tablet overlay which is supplied with AutoCAD (**Tablet.dwg** in the **Sample** folder). It is stuck down on the digitising tablet and allows picking of operations. Since the advent of Windows, the digitising tablet has decreased in popularity and been largely superseded by the mouse.

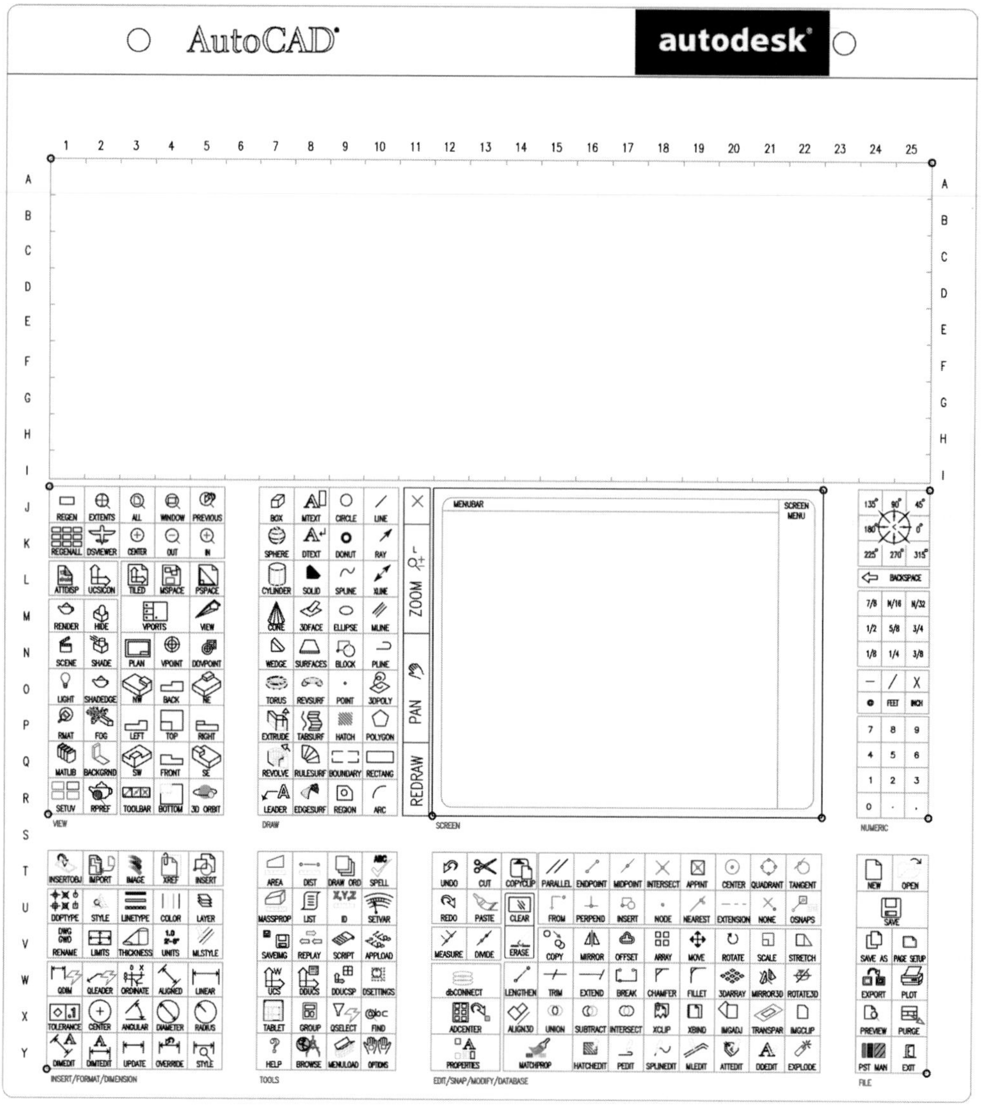

Figure 1.8. The digitising tablet overlay for AutoCAD 2005

The Text Window

The text window is similar to the command window in which you enter commands and view prompts and messages. Unlike the command window, the text window contains a complete command history for the current AutoCAD session. You can use the text window to view lengthy output from commands such as **List**, which displays detailed information about objects you select.

To display the text window while you are in the graphics area, press **F2**. The text window is displayed in front of the graphics area, as shown in Figure 1.9. If you press **F2** whilst in the text window, the graphics area is redisplayed. If the graphics area or the text window has been minimized, press **F2** to display it at its last configured size. The **F2** key functions as a toggle only if both the graphics window and the text window are open.

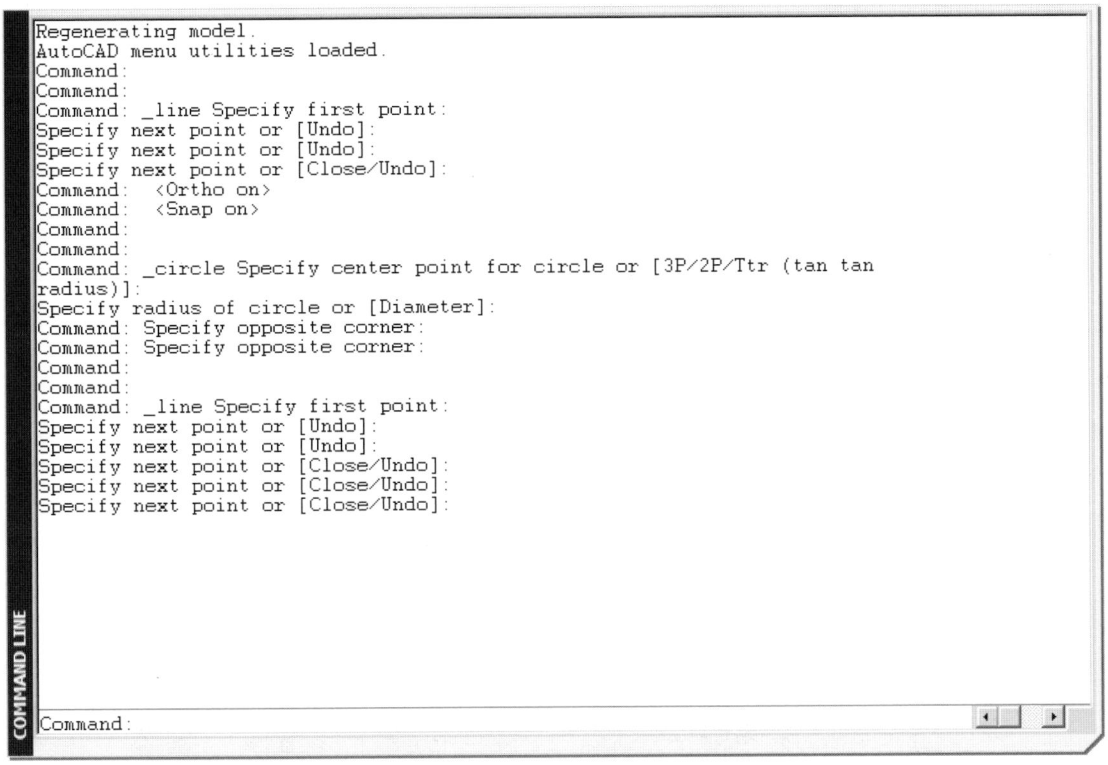

```
Regenerating model.
AutoCAD menu utilities loaded.
Command:
Command:
Command: _line Specify first point:
Specify next point or [Undo]:
Specify next point or [Undo]:
Specify next point or [Close/Undo]:
Command:  <Ortho on>
Command:  <Snap on>
Command:
Command:
Command: _circle Specify center point for circle or [3P/2P/Ttr (tan tan
radius)]:
Specify radius of circle or [Diameter]:
Command: Specify opposite corner:
Command: Specify opposite corner:
Command:
Command:
Command: _line Specify first point:
Specify next point or [Undo]:
Specify next point or [Undo]:
Specify next point or [Close/Undo]:
Specify next point or [Close/Undo]:
Specify next point or [Close/Undo]:




COMMAND LINE


Command:
```

Figure 1.9. The AutoCAD text window

Drawing in AutoCAD

In this book we shall use the following three methods for specifying coordinates.

Absolute Coordinates

With the bottom left hand corner of the drawing area being 0 in the X coordinate direction and 0 in the Y coordinate direction, you can specify coordinates in relation to that datum base point. Absolute coordinates are always entered as x,y in that order; for example

20,30

would specify a distance of 20 along the X axis (horizontally) and 30 along the Y axis (vertically), as shown in Figure 1.11.

Relative Coordinates

Relative coordinates specify a position in the X and Y axis in relation to the current position; for example

@100,0

would move the cursor to a point relative to the current position by 100 in the X axis and 0 in the Y axis. Note that relative coordinates are always preceded with the '@' sign and have the format of x,y, as shown in Figure 1.11.

Polar Coordinates

AutoCAD measures angles in an anticlockwise direction with 0° at the 3 o'clock position, as shown in Figure 1.10.

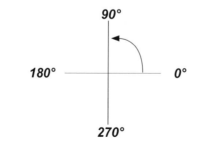

Figure 1.10. AutoCAD method of measuring angles

8

Polar coordinates are a combination of distance and angle in relation to the current position; for example

   @50<45

would produce a line with a length of 50 units at an angle of 45°. The '@' sign signifies a relative rather than absolute position, and the '<' sign signifies that what follows is an angle.

Figure 1.11 shows a combination of absolute, relative and polar coordinate entry.

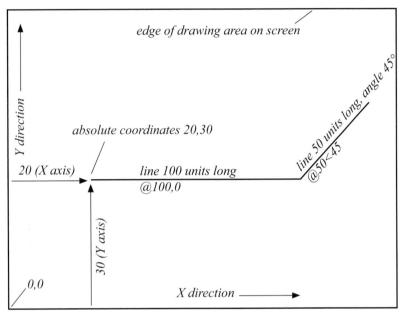

Figure 1.11. Coordinate combinations

Chapter 2 – Setting up the Drawing

Target Drawing

The target drawing is the fictitious headquarters of a small electronics company. We will build this drawing up, as shown in Figure 2.1, and continue to produce a 3D drawing, as shown in Figures 2.2 and 2.3. Lastly we will produce three different views of the drawing on a single sheet of paper with a pre-drawn border, as shown in Figure 2.4.

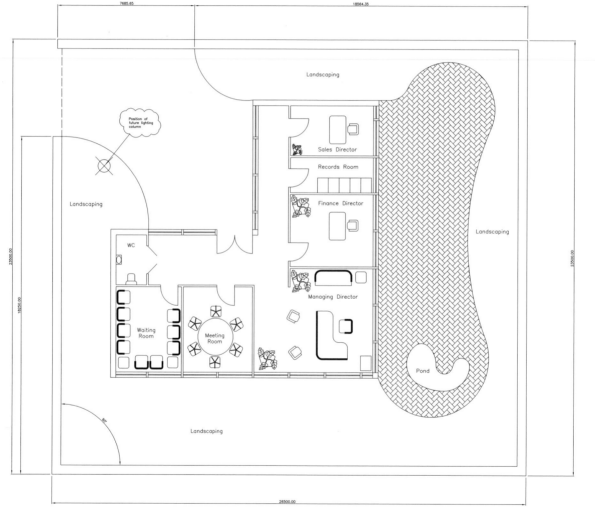

***Figure 2.1.** The 2D plan target drawing*

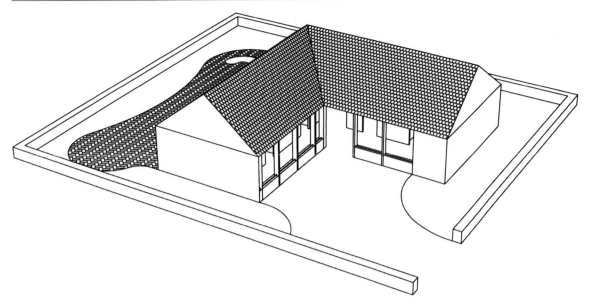

Figure 2.2. A view of the 3D model with the roof added and a height given to the boundary wall

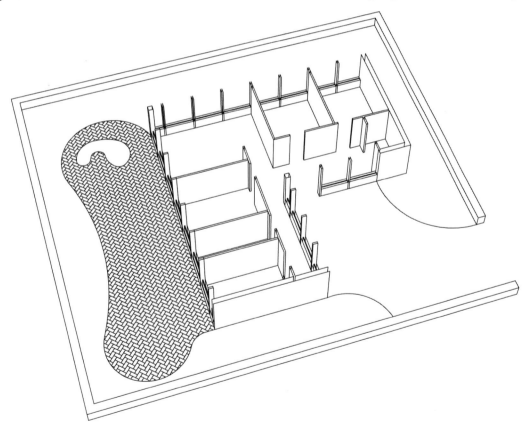

Figure 2.3. A different 3D view with the roof, text, dimension and other layers frozen

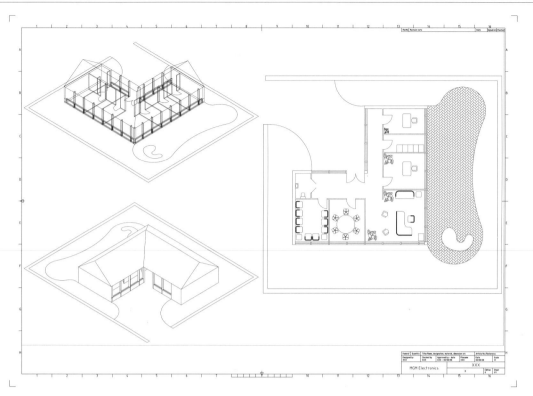

Figure 2.4. Three different views of the building on one drawing, with border information

Starting the Target Drawing

We will now start the drawing shown in Figure 2.1. If you have launched AutoCAD already, as described on page 1, click on the drop-down menu **FILE/Exit** and AutoCAD will close down.

■ Launch AutoCAD, as shown in Figure 1.1, but this time click on **Use a Wizard** in the dialogue box, as shown in Figure 2.5. This sets the units of measurement and the drawing area size.

Figure 2.5. AutoCAD 2005 Startup dialogue box with Use a Wizard and Quick Setup selected

■ Click on **Quick Setup** and then click **OK**.

The first **Quick Setup** dialogue box, which sets the unit of measurement, appears as shown in Figure 2.6(a).

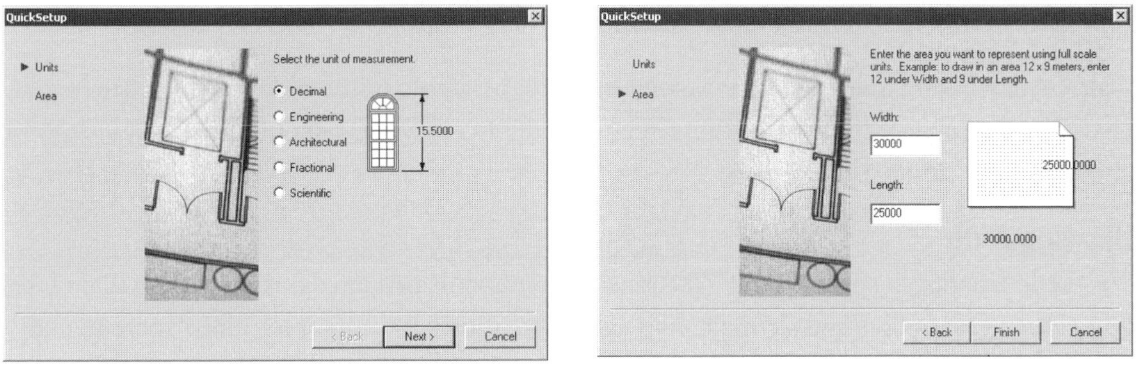

Figure 2.6. *Quick Setup dialogue boxes for setting (a) unit type and (b) drawing area*

■ Click on the **Decimal** radio button to set decimal units.

■ Click on the **Next** button.

The second **Quick Setup** dialogue box, which sets the drawing area or limits, appears as shown in Figure 2.6(b).

■ In the **Width** box enter **30000** and in the **Length** box enter **25000**, as shown in Figure 2.6(b). (For convenience, we are working in whole millimetres instead of fractional metres.)

The drawing area must be bigger than the full size of the building, because AutoCAD draws in full size on screen. Any scaling of the drawing is done at plotting time.

■ Click on **Finish**.

The drawing screen will appear, as shown in Figure 1.3. Whilst we have changed the size of the drawing area, AutoCAD still only shows the default sheet size: a portion of the drawing in the lower left corner.

*If the coordinate values do not change as you move the cursor, press **F6** to turn them on.*

We must now show all of the drawing area on screen. We do this by using the **VIEW/All** command.

- At the command line type the text shown in bold, pressing **Enter** after each entry.

Command: zoom   **Enter**

Specify corner of window, enter a scale factor (nX or nXP), or

All/Center/Dynamic/Extents/Previous/Scale(X/XP)/Window/<Realtime>: ***a***   **Enter**

AutoCAD will now regenerate the screen to show the whole of the drawing area. Move your cursor to the top right corner of the screen and the (x, y) values should now be close to or above (**30000, 25000**).

Drawing Aids

To enable drawing at speed, AutoCAD assists us with tools that aid data entry. We will now set up a screen grid of dots and a cursor snap value that allows the cursor to 'jump' incrementally in coincidence with the grid value. We can change the grid value and also make the snap value non-coincident to the grid at any time.

- From the pull-down menu use **TOOLS/Drafting Settings** and a dialogue box will appear, as shown in Figure 2.7.

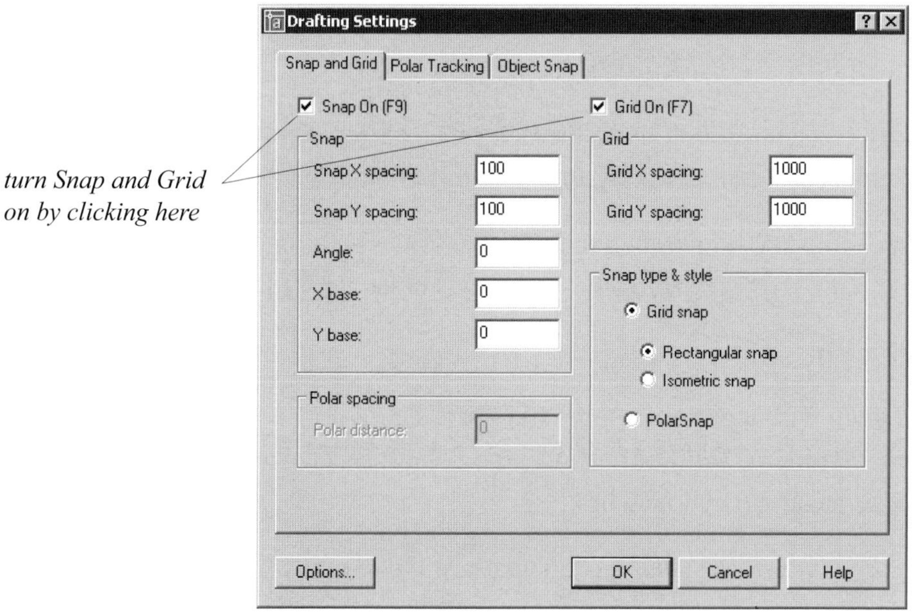

Figure 2.7. Drafting Settings dialogue box

- On the **Snap and Grid** tab, change the **Snap X spacing** to **100**.

- Change the **Grid X spacing** to **1000**.

- Turn **Snap** and **Grid** on by clicking in the **Snap On** and **Grid On** boxes.

14

■ Click on **OK**.

You do not need to change the **Y** spacing values because changing the **X** value automatically enters the **X** value into the **Y** value. The reverse is not true, so if you wanted a rectangular grid you would change the **Y** value before clicking **OK**. Figure 2.7 shows the **Drafting Settings** dialogue box with the values changed.

Precision of the Units

Even though we used the **Wizards** to specify decimal units, we were not able to set up the precision of the input; that is, to how many decimal places we need to be accurate. For distances, the nearest millimetre is adequate for this type of design, but we will use three decimal places.

■ From the pull-down menu select **FORMAT/Units** and change the precision to **three** decimal places (**0.000**) for lengths and **0** for angles, as shown in Figure 2.8.

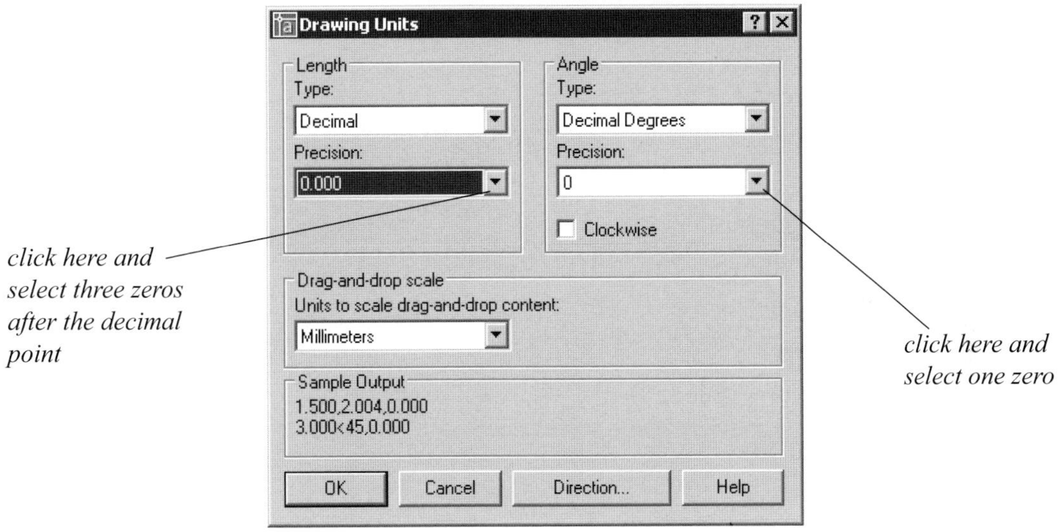

Figure 2.8. Drawing Units dialogue box

■ Click **OK** to close the dialogue box.

*Angles are measured anticlockwise with 0 degrees at the 3 o'clock position (East). Place a check in the **Clockwise** box if you want to measure angles in the opposite direction, but we shall be following the default of anticlockwise.*

Drawing Using Layers

Layering a drawing in AutoCAD is similar to using overlays in manual draughting. For example, in our target drawing all the walls are drawn on one layer and the doors on another. The roof has its own layer allocated, as does the roof tiling. At any time we can choose to conceal any of the layers so that the objects drawn on that layer are not visible on screen. If objects are not visible on screen then they will not be plotted either. If you refer to Figures 2.3 and 2.4 you will see a good example of 'freezing' or hiding layers.

Layer 0 is created by AutoCAD as the default layer and appears in every drawing. It cannot be renamed or deleted.

It is good practice to decide on your layers before you start drawing. You will probably have to add layers as you proceed, but do try to be methodical. Some of the layers for our target drawing are listed below.

Layer Name	Colour
Walls	Red
Doors	Cyan
Windows	Green
Roof	Blue
Patioedge	Yellow
Patiohatch	Magenta
Roofhatch	White
Boundary	Your Choice
Dimensions	Red
Furniture	Your Choice
Text	Cyan

To Add a New Layer

- Click on the **Layer Properties Manager** button in the **Layers** toolbar and the **Layer Properties Manager** dialogue box will appear, as shown in Figure 2.9.

- Click on the **New Layer** button, as shown in Figure 2.9. A new layer, called **Layer1**, will be added.

- Type in the name **Walls**, which will replace the name **Layer1**.

- Repeat this for all the required layers shown above. As the drawing progresses, we will add further layers.

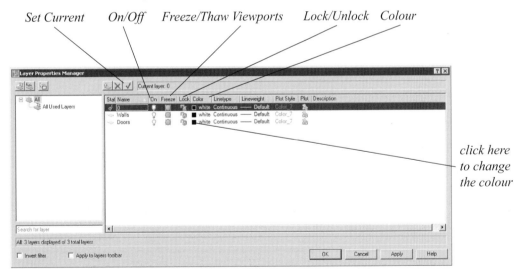

New Layer
button

Layers showing
the default layer
0, the Walls layer
already added and
Layer1 about to be
changed to layer
Doors

Figure 2.9. *Layer Properties Manager dialogue box showing default
layer 0, Walls layer, new Layer1 and the New Layer button*

*You can speed up the creation of layers by typing a comma after each layer name. As soon as
you type the comma, AutoCAD creates a new layer line and moves the cursor to it.*

Layer Colours

It is a good idea to give your layers different colours so that they become easily distinguishable
on screen and when plotted.

■ Click on the white rectangle under **Color** on the **Walls** layer, as shown in Figure 2.10
and the **Select Color** dialogue box appears.

Set Current   On/Off   Freeze/Thaw Viewports   Lock/Unlock Colour

click here
to change
the colour

Figure 2.10. *Layer Properties Manager dialogue box with Walls and Doors layers created*

- Select 'red' from the **Standard Colors** palette, as shown in Figure 2.11.

- Click **OK**. You will see that the **Walls** layer colour is now **red**.

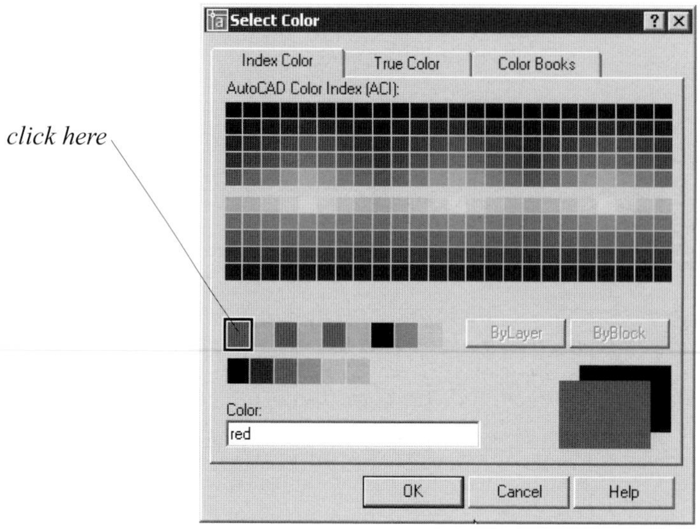

click here

Figure 2.11. Select Color dialogue box with the colour red chosen for the Walls layer

- Repeat this operation for all of the layers giving them their colours as listed on page 16.

- Highlight the **Walls** layer by clicking on the word '**Walls**', then select the **Set Current** button, as shown in Figure 2.10.

*This changes the active layer to the **Walls** layer in preparation for the building outline.*

- Click **OK** to close the **Layer Properties Manager** dialogue box.

- The **Layers** toolbar should now show the word **Walls** with the layer colour, as shown in Figure 2.12.

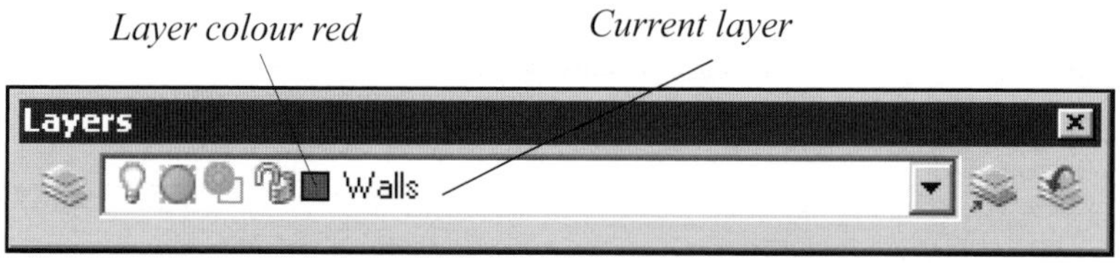

Layer colour red   *Current layer*

Figure 2.12. Layers toolbar showing the current layer and its colour

Saving Drawings

It is good practice to save your drawing every ten minutes or so, as you proceed, rather than when you finish drawing. It is also good practice to create a folder for your drawings.

- Click on the **Save** button and the **Save Drawing As** dialogue box will appear, as shown in Figure 2.13.

- If you are saving the drawing to the floppy drive click on the **Save in** pull-down menu and click on **3½ Floppy [A:]**.

- Click on the **Create New Folder** button, as shown in Figure 2.13.

- The words **New Folder** will appear, highlighted. Overtype with a folder name of your choice. Figure 2.13 shows a new folder called '**drawings**'.

- Double click on your new folder name. The new folder name will appear in the **Save in** window, as shown in Figure 2.13.

The drawing does not have a name yet and AutoCAD automatically inserts the filename as **'Drawing'**.

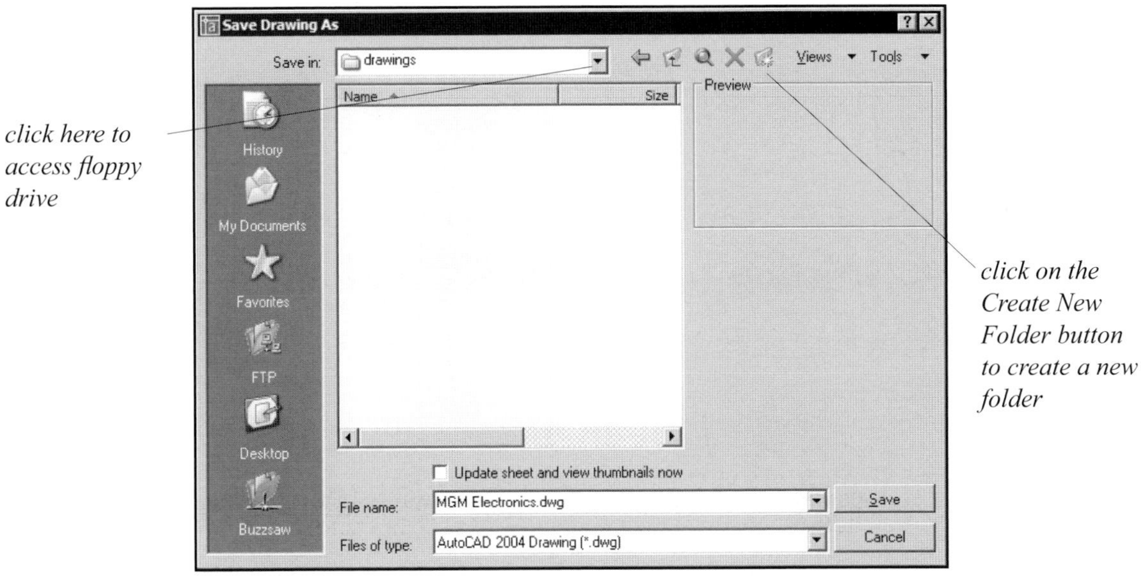

click here to access floppy drive

click on the Create New Folder button to create a new folder

Figure 2.13. The Save Drawing As dialogue box

- Overtype the word '**Drawing**' with '**MGM Electronics**' and click on **Save**.

The drawing is now saved up to this point. When you save your drawing for the first time the '**Save Drawing As**'dialogue box will appear; after that, clicking on the **Save** button (quick save) does not produce a dialogue box but does save the drawing.

Chapter 3 – Drawing the Building

SNAP

We will leave the grid visible but turn **Snap** off initially, although it is not essential to do so. Can you remember how to toggle **Snap** off using the keyboard? Try **F9**.

We are now ready to design the headquarters of MGM Electronics.

Instead of using the F9 key, you could click the Snap button on the Status bar.

We will use **absolute coordinates** to draw the outline of the building, as shown in Figure 3.1.

Drawing

■ Use **DRAW/Line** from the drop-down menu and type, at the Command line, the text shown in bold text only. Press **Enter** after each input.

Type U for Undo at the Command line to retrace your steps if you make errors.

Command: _line Specify first point:	**5000,6000**	**Enter**
Specify next point or [Undo]:	**20000,6000**	**Enter**
Specify next pointor or [Undo]:	**20000,21000**	**Enter**
Specify next point or [Close/Undo]:	**13000,21000**	**Enter**
Specify next point or [Close/Undo]:	**13000,14000**	**Enter**
Specify next point or [Close/Undo]:	**5000,14000**	**Enter**
Specify next point or [Close/Undo]:	**5000,6000**	**Enter**
Specify next point or [Close/Undo]:	**Enter**	

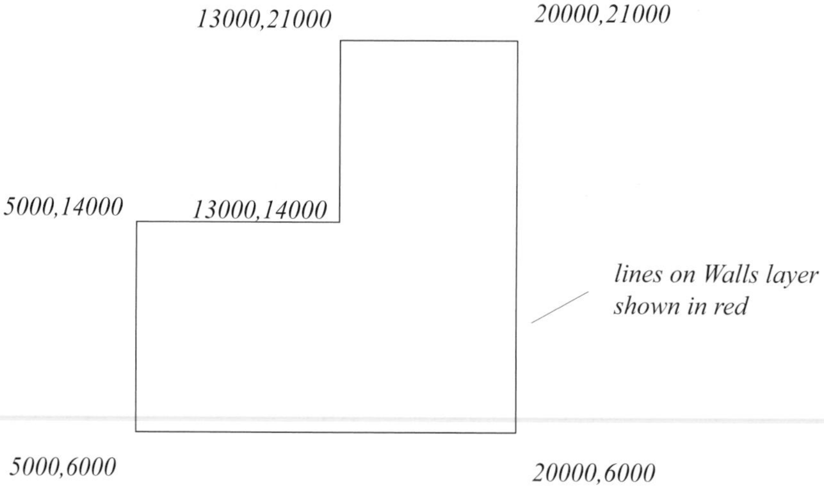

13000,21000   *20000,21000*

5000,14000   *13000,14000*

lines on Walls layer shown in red

5000,6000   *20000,6000*

Figure 3.1. *The building outline*

We will now draw the inner lines of the exterior wall, as shown in Figure 3.2. The wall width is 300mm. Can you calculate what the absolute coordinates will be? If you are having difficulty the answer is below.

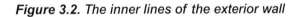

*Remember that you can repeat the previous command by pressing **Enter** or the **Spacebar** on the keyboard, or clicking the **right button** on the mouse (if you have customised the right-click settings).*

Command: _line Specify first point:	**5300,6300**	**Enter**
Specify next point or [Undo]:	**19700,6300**	**Enter**
Specify next point or [Undo]:	**19700,20700**	**Enter**
Specify next point or [Close/Undo]:	**13300,20700**	**Enter**
Specify next pointor [Close/Undo]:	**13300,13700**	**Enter**
Specify next point or [Close/Undo]:	**5300,13700**	**Enter**
Specify next point or [Close/Undo]:	**5300,6300**	**Enter**
Specify next point or [Close/Undo]:	**Enter**	

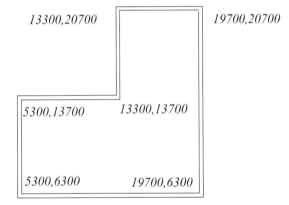

Figure 3.2. *The inner lines of the exterior wall*

■ For the inner partition walls we will draw with **relative coordinates** but start with an **absolute coordinate**, as shown in Figure 3.3.

Command: _line Specify first point:	**5000,11000**	**Enter**
Specify next point or [Undo]:	**@10000,0**	**Enter**
Specify next point or [Undo]:	**@0,9700**	**Enter**
Specify next point or [Close/Undo]:	**Enter**	

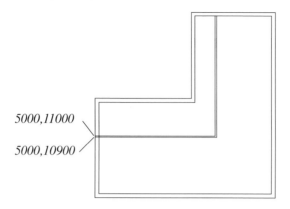

5000,11000

5000,10900

Figure 3.3. *Drawing the partition walls*

■ Press the **Spacebar** to repeat the **Line** command.

Command: _line Specify first point:	**5000,10900**	***Enter***
Specify next point or [Undo]:	**@10100,0**	***Enter***
Specify next pointor [Undo]:	**@0,9800**	***Enter***
Specify next point or [Close/Undo]:	***Enter***	

*To check a coordinate value, enter **ID** at the command line and press **Enter**. When asked to **Specify a Point** move the cursor to the end of a line in the drawing and click the left mouse button. The command line will show the value for the **X**, **Y** and **Z** coordinates. The **Z** value will always be **0** in a 2D drawing.*

Next, we will add the partitions separating the rooms, again starting with an **absolute coordinate**, as shown in Figure 3.4.

Command: _line Specify first point:	**9000,6300**	***Enter***
Specify next point or [Undo]:	**@0,4600**	***Enter***
Specify next point or [Undo]:	***Enter***	

■ Press the **Enter** key to repeat the **Line** command

Command: _line Specify first point:	**9100,6300**	***Enter***
Specify next point or [Undo]:	**@0,4600**	***Enter***
Specify next point or [Undo]:	***Enter***	

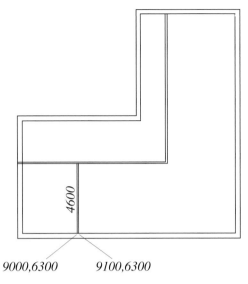

Figure 3.4. Internal partition wall

■ The remaining partitions are shown in Figure 3.5. Starting with **absolute coordinates**, draw the room partitions. Can you draw them by calculating the **relative coordinates**? All of the partition widths are 100mm. **Save** the drawing when you have finished.

Remember that when using relative coordinates, drawing in a negative direction (right to left (x) or top to bottom (y)) will mean that the coordinate must be preceded by a – (minus).

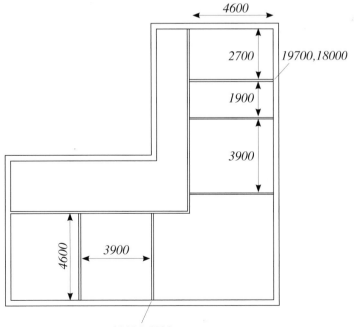

Figure 3.5. Partition wall dimensions

Enlarging the View of the Drawing (the Zoom Command)

We now need to create the door openings. These are 1000mm wide, except for the double doors. To create these accurately it is better for us to have an enlarged view of the drawing and move around the drawing in that view. AutoCAD provides a tool called **Zoom** which allows us to specify an area of the drawing on which we want to work.

You can use the **Zoom** command by selecting **VIEW/Zoom** from the pull-down menu or with the **Zoom/Window** button on the **Standard** toolbar, but we will load the **Zoom** toolbar so that you become familiar with the process of loading toolbars.

- From the pull-down menu select **VIEW/Toolbars**. The **Customize** dialogue box will appear with its **Toolbars** tab selected, as shown in Figure 3.6.

- Scroll down and place a check in the **Zoom** box, then click on **Close**.

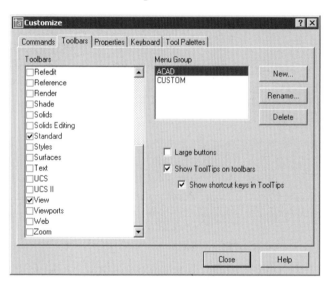
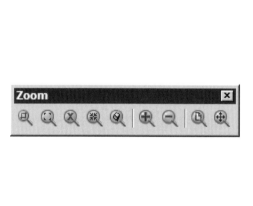

Figure 3.6. The Customize dialogue box and the loaded Zoom toolbar

The toolbar appears on screen as a **floating toolbar**, which can be moved anywhere around the screen by clicking and holding down the left mouse button on the blue area. The toolbar can also be **docked** at the sides of the screen, which is convenient as it does not interfere with the view of the drawing.

- Click on the **Zoom Window** tool in the **Zoom** toolbar (or use **VIEW/Zoom/Window** from the drop-down menu) and form a rectangle with your cursor by picking two diagonally opposite corners of the rectangular area, as shown in Figure 3.7. It is shown shaded here for clarity only. Figure 3.9 shows the new view of the drawing.

Modifying the Drawing

If you look at the enlarged view in Figure 3.9 you will see that the corridor partition lines overlap the left hand wall and touch the outer wall; this is the way that we drew it. We need to correct this with the commands **MODIFY/Trim** and **MODIFY/Break**. We now need to load the **Modify** toolbar.

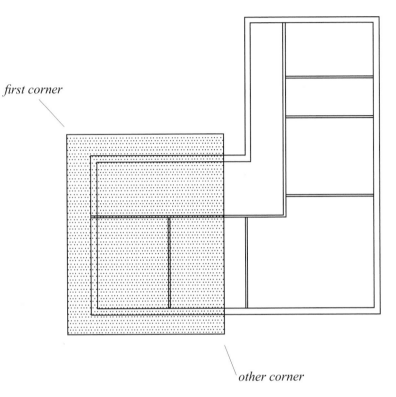

first corner

other corner

Figure 3.7. Zoom window area

- Using the same method as we used for loading the **Zoom** toolbar, load the **Modify** toolbar (not **Modify II**). (You may find that it is already loaded.)

The toolbar will appear within your drawing area, as shown in Figure 3.8, with the icons all on one line. You have the option of leaving it where it appears, but it is more convenient to dock it to the left, right or top of the drawing area.

- To move the toolbar click on a part of the toolbar outside the button commands and drag it to its destination, as shown in Figure 3.8. On the perimeter of the screen it will adopt the shape of the toolbar closest to it, but the contents remain the same.

- You can do the same for the **Zoom** toolbar also.

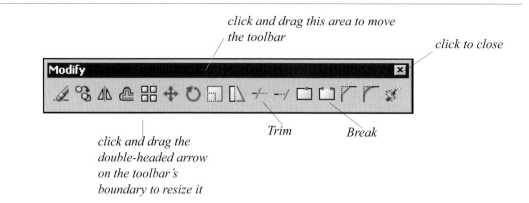

click and drag this area to move
the toolbar

click to close

click and drag the
double-headed arrow
on the toolbar's
boundary to resize it

Trim   Break

Figure 3.8. The Modify toolbar

SNAP   ■   Ensure that **Snap** is on.

■   Select **MODIFY/Trim**. (Note how the cursor changed to a square 'pickbox', as shown in Figure 3.9).

Command: _trim

Current settings: Projection=UCS, Edge=None

Select cutting edges ...   **(Select vertical inner wall as cutting edge as shown in Figure 3.9)**

Select objects: 1 found

Select objects: **Enter**

Select object to trim or shift-select to extend or [Project/Edge/Undo]:   **(Select overlapping line)**

Select object to trim or shift-select to extend or [Project/Edge/Undo]:   **(Select overlapping line)**

Select object to trim or shift-select to extend or [Project/Edge/Undo]   **Enter**

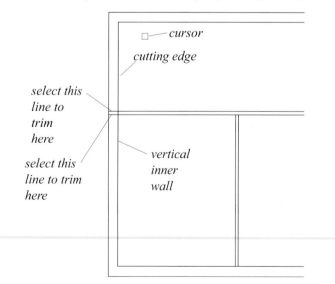

cursor

cutting edge

select this
line to
trim
here

select this
line to trim
here

vertical
inner
wall

Figure 3.9. The new view using the Zoom command, with the Trim command in progress

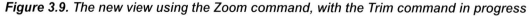

The modified drawing should now look the same as Figure 3.10.

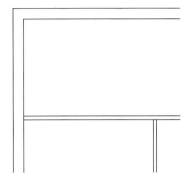

Figure 3.10. The completed Trim command

We now need to use **MODIFY/Break** to erase the inner line of the outer wall where the newly trimmed partition lines touch it. This command splits a line into two portions, or forms a gap between two chosen points.

- Remember that **Snap** is on, so the cursor will 'jump' from the first break point to the second break point because the Snap value is set to **100** (see Chapter 2, Figure 2.7).

- Click the **Break** button from the **Modify** toolbar (you could also use the drop-down menu **MODIFY/Break**) and the command line will prompt

Command: _break Select object:	*(Select line, as shown in Figure 3.11)*
Specify second point [or First point]:	*f Enter*
Specify first break point:	*(Select point, as shown in Figure 3.11)*
Specify second break point:	*(Select point, as shown in Figure 3.11)*

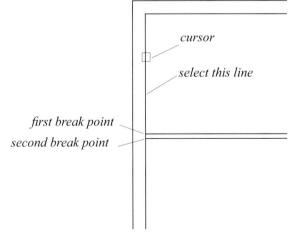

Figure 3.11. The Break command in progress

The completed break is shown in Figure 3.12.

Figure 3.12. The completed Break command

*Remember that if you make a mistake at any point, type **U** for Undo and it will take you back one step.*

Closing a Toolbar

■ From the pull-down menu select **VIEW/Toolbars** and click off the **Zoom** toolbar that we loaded earlier, or pick the **Close** button on the toolbar itself, as shown in Figure 3.8.

Whenever we use **Zoom** from now on we will use the existing **Zoom** button from the **Standard** toolbar at the top of the screen.

Note that it is slightly different from the **Zoom** button which we loaded. It has an arrow in the bottom right hand corner which indicates that it is part of a 'flyout': clicking and holding the cursor on this will activate the remainder of the **Zoom** buttons, as shown in Figure 3.13.

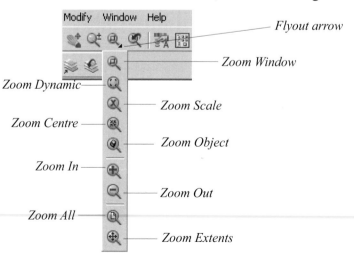

Figure 3.13. The Zoom flyout

Adding the Door Openings

*Remember that we set the **Snap** value to 100 so your cursor will 'jump' every 100 units.*

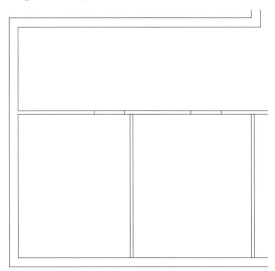

■ Ensure that **Snap** is still on. If not, turn it on with **F9**.

■ If the **Grid** is off, turn it on with **F7**.

■ Ensure that **Object Snap** (**OSNAP**) is off.

■ Using **DRAW/Line** draw in the door openings, 1000mm wide, as shown in Figure 3.14. Because **Grid** and **Snap** are on, you will not need coordinates.

Figure 3.14. The door reveals shown in the enlarged view

Moving Around the Drawing (the Pan Command)

After you have drawn the door reveals in Figure 3.14 use **Pan Realtime** to move around the drawing.

■ Select **Pan**, and click and drag the drawing area to move it to the required position.

■ Press **Esc** or **Enter**.

- Complete the remaining 1000mm wide door openings, as in Figure 3.15. The positioning of the openings is not critical so use your own judgement.

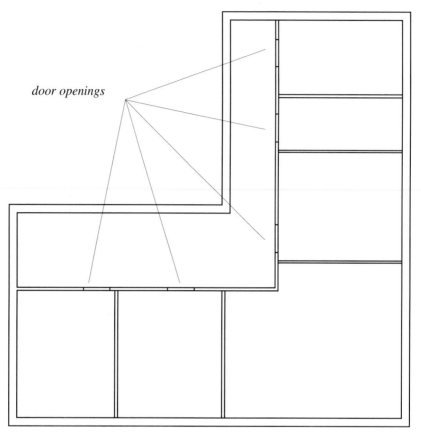

door openings

Figure 3.15. *The completed door reveals*

Modifying the Drawing (the Break Command)

After completing the door reveals we now need to remove the lines between them to complete the door openings and open up the partition walls.

- Ensure that **Snap** is still on. (Snap will appear as 'recessed' on the **Status bar** if it is on).

- **Pan** to the area shown in Figure 3.16.

■ Click the **Break** button from the **Modify** toolbar (you could instead use pull-down menu **MODIFY/Break**) and the command line will prompt

Command: _break Select object:	***(Select line, as shown in Figure 3.16)***
Enter second break point [or First point]:	***f*** ***Enter***
Specify first break point:	***(Select first point, as shown in Figure 3.16)***
Specify second break point:	***(Select second point, as shown in Figure 3.16)***

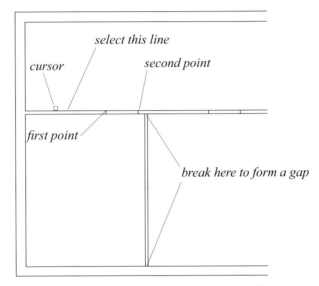

Figure 3.16. The Modify/Break command

■ Repeat the **Break** command (press the **Spacebar**) for the second opening on the same line and again for the line of the partition below it. Your drawing should now look like Figure 3.17. Complete the remainder of the doorways and partition wall junctions.

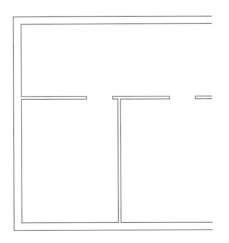

Figure 3.17. The completed doorways and walls

Modifying the Drawing (the Extend command)

To correctly form the double doorway to the Managing Director's office we must first extend one line to another to form the reveal, as shown in Figure 3.18.

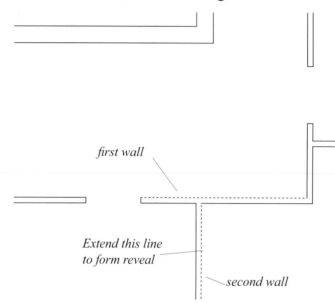

first wall

Extend this line to form reveal

second wall

Figure 3.18. Using the Extend command to form the door reveal

■ From the **Modify** toolbar pick **Extend** and the command line will prompt

Command: _extend

Current settings: Projection=UCS, Edge=None

Select boundary edges ...

Select objects: 1 found   **(Select first wall, as shown in Figure 3.18)**

Select objects: **Enter**

Select object to extend or shift-select to trim or [Project/Edge/Undo]:   **(Select second wall)**

Select object to extend or shift-select to trim or [Project/Edge/Undo]:   **Enter**

The walls will now look like Figure 3.19.

■ Repeat the **Extend** command for the other side of the double door. The result will be as shown in Figure 3.20.

32

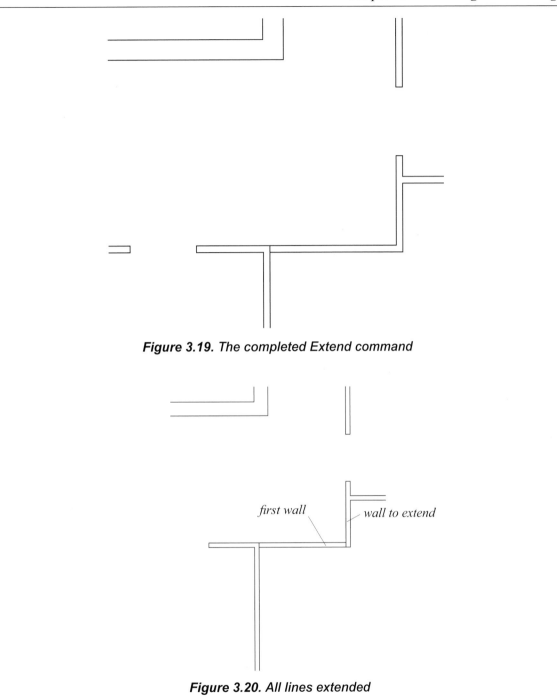

Figure 3.19. *The completed Extend command*

first wall

wall to extend

Figure 3.20. *All lines extended*

`SNAP` ■ Ensure that **Snap** is still **On**.

■ Use **MODIFY/Break** to form the door opening to the Managing Director's office and complete it, as shown in Figure 3.21.

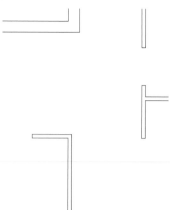

Figure 3.21. The completed doorway to the Managing Director's office

We now need to form the main doorway to the building.

`GRID` ■ Ensure that **Grid** is still **On**. (**Grid** will appear as 'recessed' on the **Status bar** if it is on).

■ Use **Pan** and **Zoom Window** to show a view similar to Figure 3.22.

■ Use **MODIFY/Extend** to extend the external wall, as shown in Figure 3.22.

■ Use **DRAW/Line** to draw in the left hand door reveal and the window reveal, as shown in Figure 3.22.

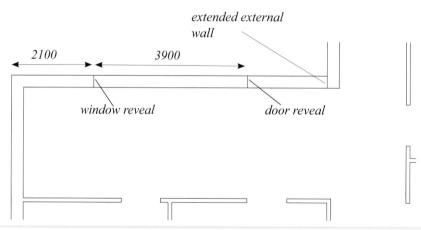

Figure 3.22. The main doorway and front window reveal

- Use **MODIFY/Break** to erase the lines in between the new door reveal and the extended wall line.

Figure 3.23 shows the new doorway.

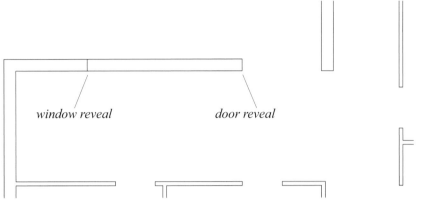

Figure 3.23. The new front doorway after the Break command

- Use **VIEW/Zoom/Extents** (which will show the extents of what is drawn on screen) to show a view similar to Figure 3.24, which shows the completed drawing so far.

- **Save** the drawing.

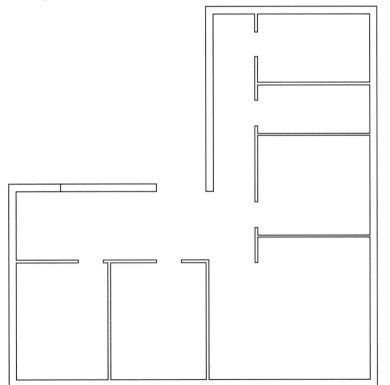

Figure 3.24. The completed drawing so far

Chapter 4 – Drawing the Windows

We have finished drawing the walls. Before we place the windows we have to make the **Windows** layer the **Current** layer.

Changing Layers

- Click on the **Layer Properties Manager** button in the **Layers** toolbar and the **Layer Properties Manager** dialogue box will appear, as shown in Figure 4.1.

- Click on the layer named **Windows** and make it the drawing layer by clicking on **Set Current** (the green tick button).

- Click on **OK**.

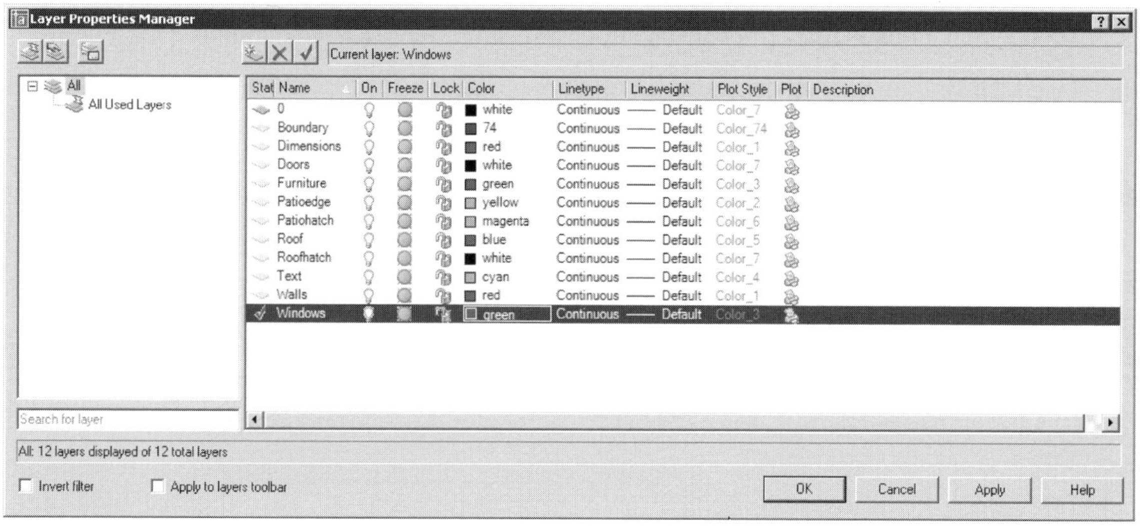

Figure 4.1. The Layer Properties Manager dialogue box with the Windows layer current

The **Layers** toolbar should now be similar to that shown in Figure 4.2 with the **Windows** layer **Current** and shown as green.

- Use **VIEW/Zoom/Window** to obtain a view similar to Figure 4.3.

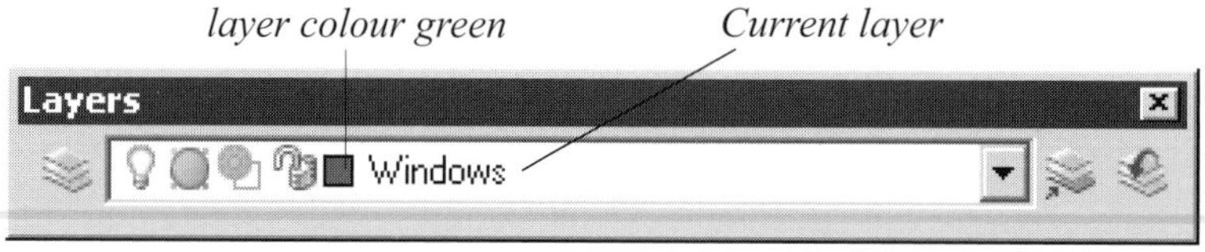

Figure 4.2. Layers Toolbar showing the Current layer and its colour

■ Ensure that **Snap** and **Grid** are still on.

■ Use **DRAW/Line** to draw in the 100mm-wide mullion separating the window openings, as shown in Figure 4.3.

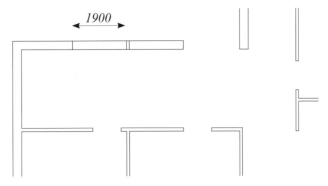

Figure 4.3. Window mullion in the front wall

■ Use **Pan** and **Zoom Window** to show a view similar to Figure 4.4.

■ Use **DRAW/Line** to draw in the 100mm-wide window mullion at the building rear, as shown in Figure 4.4.

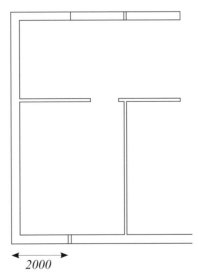

Figure 4.4. The first window mullion at the rear of the building

Copying Objects (the Array Command)

You can copy an object or selection set in polar or rectangular arrays. A **polar** array controls the number of copies of the object about a chosen point and whether the copies are rotated. A **rectangular** array controls the number of rows and columns and the distance between them. We are going to copy the window mullion along the rear wall using the **MODIFY/Array** command. The distance between the mullions is 2000mm and we will use a **rectangular** array.

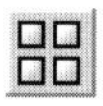

■ Use **MODIFY/Array** and the **Array** dialogue box will appear, as shown in Figure 4.5.

■ Click on the **Rectangular Array** radio button.

■ Enter **1 Row** and **7 Columns**.

■ Enter the **Column offset** as **2000**.

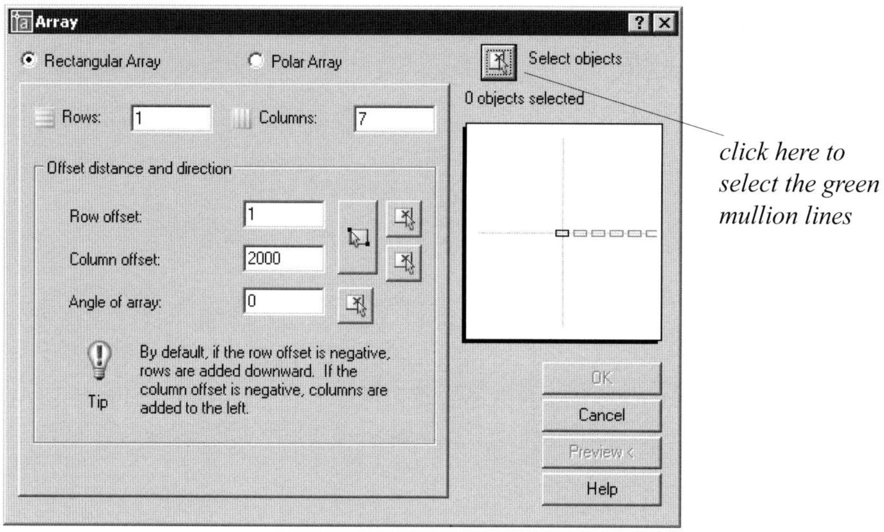

click here to select the green mullion lines

Figure 4.5. The Array dialogue box with a Rectangular Array of 1 Row and 7 Columns

■ Click on **Select objects** to choose the items to be arrayed.

■ The **Array** dialogue box will disappear and the Command line will show

Command:_array	
Select objects:	**(Pick a mullion line, as shown in Figure 4.6)**
Select objects: 1 found, 2 total	**(Pick the second mullion line, as shown in Figure 4.6)**
Select objects:	**Enter**

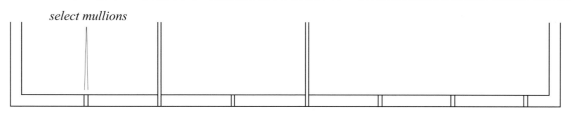

Figure 4.6. *The completed window mullions using the Rectangular Array command*

- The **Array** dialogue box will reappear.

- Click **OK** in the **Array** dialogue box and the mullions are repeated seven times with a distance of 2000mm between them.

- You will now need to **Pan** across the drawing to the corner of the side wall so that we can draw the first 100mm mullion in the vertical direction, as shown in Figure 4.7.

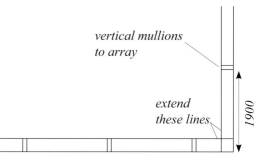

Figure 4.7. *The extended walls and the first mullion on the rear wall*

- However, before drawing the mullion, use the **MODIFY/Extend** command to extend the rear walls, as shown in Figure 4.7. Although the layer **Windows** is **Current**, extending the walls will draw those lines on their own layer, **Walls**.

*Whilst using the **MODIFY/Extend** command you can switch to the **MODIFY/Trim** command by holding down the **Shift** key as you select the objects to **Extend**. You can also follow the same procedure whilst in the **MODIFY/Trim** command to switch to **MODIFY/Extend**.*

We need to break the extended lines at the **Intersection** of the inner wall and where they touch the outer walls, as shown in Figure 4.7, to enable us to change the height of the walls later in Chapter 9.

You will not see anything happening to the wall, as the **Break** command simply splits it.

SNAP ■ Ensure that **Snap** is still on.

■ From the **MODIFY** toolbar pick **Break** and the command line will prompt

Command: _break Select object: *(Select inner horizontal wall, as shown in Figure 4.8)*

Enter second point (or F for first point):   *f*   *Enter*

Enter first point: *(Select junction A, as shown in Figure 4.8)*

Enter second point: *@ (breaks at the previous point chosen)*   *Enter*

■ Repeat the **Break** command, breaking the outer horizontal wall at point **B**, the inner vertical wall at point **A**, and the outer vertical wall at point **C**, as shown in Figure 4.8.

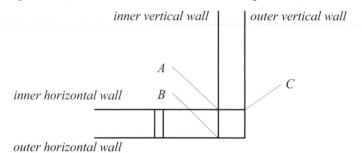

inner vertical wall   *outer vertical wall*

A

C

inner horizontal wall   *B*

outer horizontal wall

Figure 4.8. The Break command used to break at the points shown

■ Use **DRAW/Line** to draw in the 100mm-wide window mullion, as shown in Figure 4.7, 1900mm from the building corner.

We will now **MODIFY/Array** the mullion, but this time in a vertical row rather than a column. Figures 4.6 and 4.7 show the horizontal and vertical mullions which we have drawn up to this point.

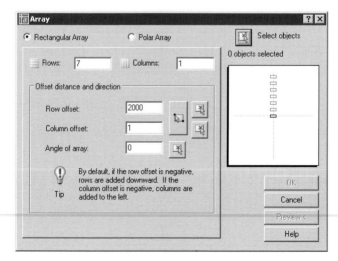

Figure 4.9. The Array dialogue box with a Rectangular Array of 7 Rows and 1 Column

- Use **MODIFY/Array** and the **Array** dialogue box will appear, as shown in Figure 4.9.

- Click on the **Rectangular Array** radio button.

- This time enter **7 Rows** and **1 Column**.

- Enter the **Row offset** as **2000**. (The **Column offset** doesn't matter, as there is only one column.)

- Click on **Select objects** to choose the items to be arrayed.

- The **Array** dialogue box will disappear and the Command line will show

Command:_array	
Select objects:	**(Pick a mullion line, as shown in Figure 4.10)**
Select objects: 1 found, 2 total	**(Pick the second mullion line, as shown in Figure 4.10)**
Select objects:	**Enter**

- The **Array** dialogue box will reappear. Click **OK** and the mullions are again repeated seven times with a distance of 2000mm between them.

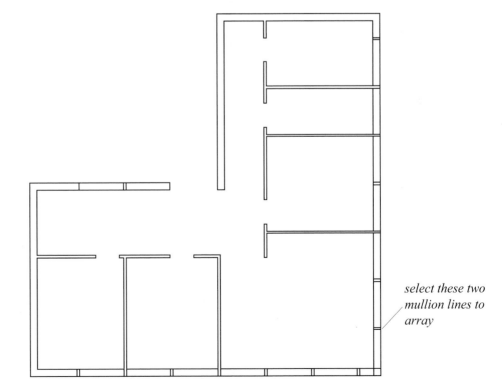

select these two mullion lines to array

Figure 4.10. The window mullions after arraying vertically

SNAP ■ Ensure that **Snap** is still on and **Pan** to the area shown in Figure 4.12.

■ Use **DRAW/Line** to draw the 100mm mullion in the front wall, as shown in Figure 4.12, 2000mm from the building corner.

We will use **MODIFY/Array** to array these two lines. The difference this time is that we will array in a negative direction (downwards) so the distance between rows will be preceded with a minus sign.

■ Use **MODIFY/Array** and the **Array** dialogue box will appear, as shown in Figure 4.11.

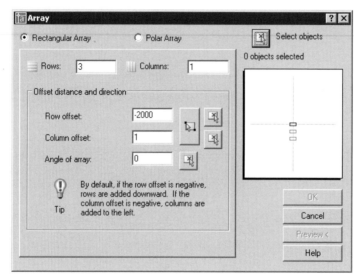

Figure 4.11. The Array command on the mullions in the front wall with a negative Row offset

■ Ensure that the **Rectangular Array** radio button is selected.

■ This time enter **3 Rows** and **1 Column**.

■ Enter the **Row offset** as **−2000** (don't forget the minus), as shown in **Figure 4.11**.

■ Click on **Select objects**, and complete the process as you did earlier.

■ **MODIFY/Extend** the inner wall line to meet the outer lines, as shown in Figure 4.12.

■ **Save** the drawing.

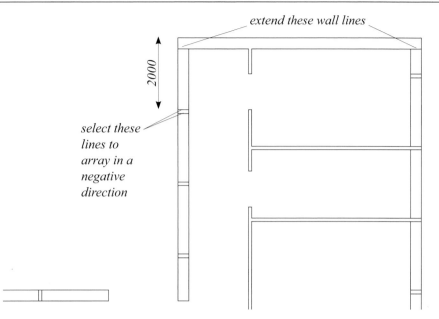

Figure 4.12. *The result of the Array command on the mullions in the front wall*

Drawing with Object Snap

So far we have relied upon a **Snap** value, and for **Snap** to be turned on, for drawing to be carried out accurately. We can also snap to a location which may not coincide with the **Grid** or **Snap** setting.

■ Use **VIEW**/**Toolbars** from the pull-down menu to load the **Object Snap** toolbar, which appears as shown in Figure 4.13.

■ Move it to a location on the screen suitable for you.

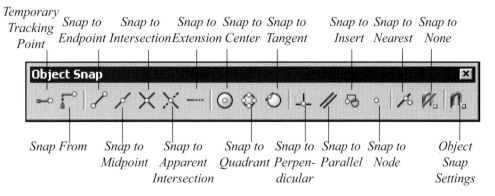

Figure 4.13. *The Object Snap toolbar*

The **Object Snap** toolbar lets you enter an Osnap mode temporarily, so that you can select a point for the current command. For example, if you are drawing a line and need to specify that the first point is the midpoint of another line, you can press **Snap to Midpoint**; the Command window changes to **Command: _line Specify first point: _mid of** and as you move your cursor it will snap to the midpoints of the objects nearby. As soon as you have clicked on a point, the Osnap mode will no longer be in force.

If you want to make an object snap permanently available, or you want to use more than one object snap at the same time, use **TOOLS/Drafting Settings**. Click the **Object Snap** tab and under **Object Snap modes** place checks in the boxes, as shown in Figure 4.14. Click on **OK**.

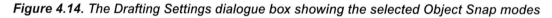

Figure 4.14. The Drafting Settings dialogue box showing the selected Object Snap modes

To cycle through the object snaps you have chosen, use the **Tab** key during a command; in the example shown in Figure 4.14, **Tab** will alternate between **Endpoint** and **Midpoint**.

Drawing the Glazing

We are now ready to draw the lines that represent the glazing.

SNAP ■ Ensure that **Snap** is set to **Off**.

■ Firstly, **Zoom** and **Pan** to the area shown in Figure 4.15.

■ **MODIFY/Extend** the wall, as shown in Figures 4.15 and 4.16.

■ Use **DRAW/Line** from the **Midpoint** of the first mullion to the **Midpoint** of the second mullion, as shown in Figure 4.15. The command line will prompt

Command: _line Specify first point: ___mid of (Pick as shown in Figure 4.15)__

Specify next point or [Undo]:   ___mid of (Pick as shown in Figure 4.15)__

Specify next point or [Undo]:   __Enter__

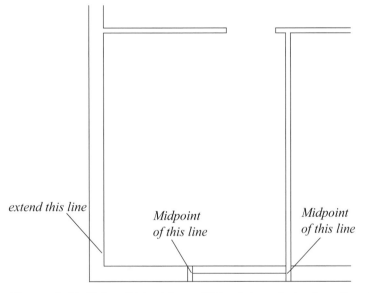

extend this line

*Midpoint
of this line*

*Midpoint
of this line*

Figure 4.15. Using Object Snap Midpoint mode to draw the glazing line

Copying with the Offset Command

We will now create two copies of the line, 20mm above and below it, with the **MODIFY/ Offset** command. Then we will erase the original line so the two new lines form the actual impression of the glass thickness, as shown in Figure 4.17.

You may need to use **VIEW/Zoom/Window** to enlarge the area first.

■ Use **MODIFY/Offset** and the command line will prompt

Command: _offset

Specify offset distance or [Through] <Through>:   **20**   **Enter**

Select object to offset or <exit>:   **(Select glazing line as drawn in Figure 4.16)**

Specify point on side to offset: **(Pick anywhere above the line)**

Select object to offset or <exit>:   **(Select the line again)**

Specify point on side to offset: **(Pick anywhere below the line)**

Select object to offset or <exit>:   **Enter**

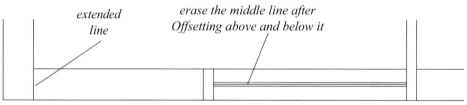

Figure 4.16. Offsetting and Erasing the middle line

■ **MODIFY/Erase** the middle line, as shown in Figure 4.16; the result is as shown in Figure 4.17. You may need to use **VIEW/Zoom/Window** to enlarge the area to pick the middle line.

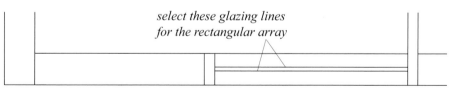

Figure 4.17. The result of Offsetting and Erasing the middle line

We can now use the **MODIFY/Array** command to copy the glazing in between the mullions. The process is exactly the same as we used to copy the mullions (see page 38) but there are six columns instead of seven.

■ Use **MODIFY/Array** and the Array dialogue box will appear, as shown in Figure 4.18.

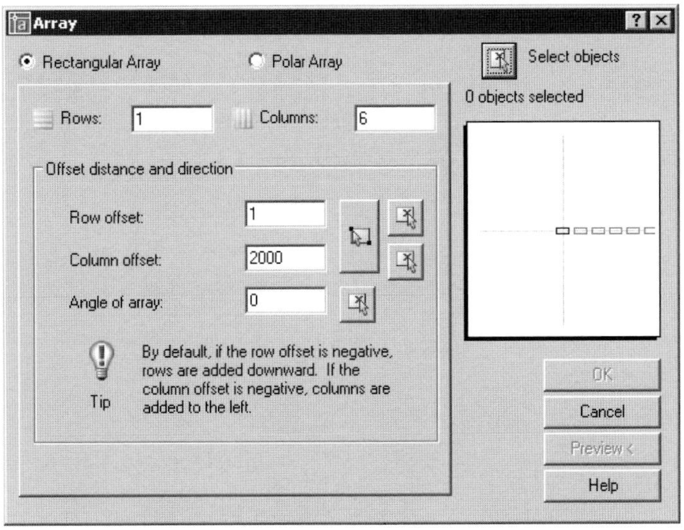

Figure 4.18. The Array command on the glazing

- Ensure that the **Rectangular Array** radio button is selected.

- This time enter **1 Row** and **6 Columns**.

- Enter the **Column offset** as **2000**.

- Click on **Select objects** to choose the items to be arrayed, as shown in Figure 4.17.

- The **Array** dialogue box will disappear. Complete the process as you did earlier.

*You will probably need to use **VIEW/Zoom/Out** to see the result of the array, as shown in Figure 4.19.*

- Use **VIEW/Zoom/Window** to zoom to the area shown in Figure 4.19 adjacent to the front door.

- Turn **Snap** on.

- **MODIFY/Offset** the wall line upwards by 300mm, as shown in Figure 4.19.

- Use **MODIFY/Break** to break the two vertical lines at the junction of the new line, as shown in Figure 4.19. This action is in preparation for converting the drawing to 3D in Chapter 9.

Remember to use @ as the second break point.

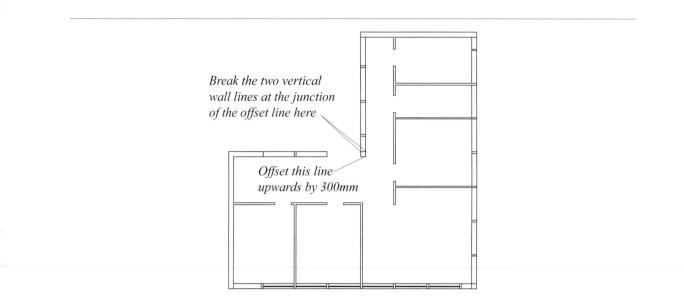

Break the two vertical wall lines at the junction of the offset line here

Offset this line upwards by 300mm

Figure 4.19. The result of the Array command on the glazing

- To create the glazing along the rear wall, **Pan** to the area shown in Figure 4.20 and draw a line from the **Midpoints** between the mullions. Turn **Snap Off**.

- Use **MODIFY/Offset** to produce the glazing lines as before.

- **MODIFY/Erase** the central line, as shown in Figure 4.20.

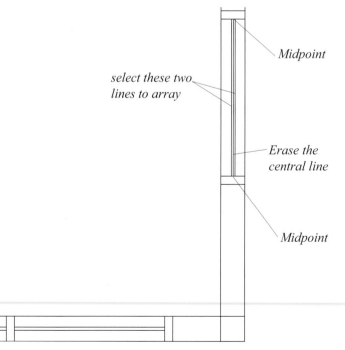

Midpoint

select these two lines to array

Erase the central line

Midpoint

Figure 4.20. The first line of glazing in the rear wall

■ Use **MODIFY/Array** to copy the glazing in between the mullions; the **Array** dialogue box will appear, as shown in Figure 4.21.

■ Ensure that the **Rectangular Array** radio button is selected.

■ Enter **6 Rows** and **1 Column**.

■ Enter the **Row offset** as **2000**.

■ Click on **Select objects** to choose the two lines of glazing, then press **Enter**. Click **OK**.

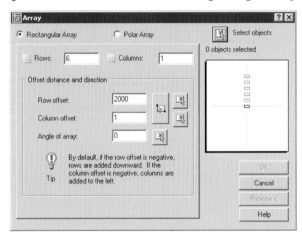

Figure 4.21. The Array command on the glazing in the rear wall

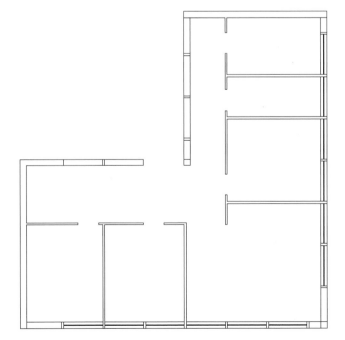

Figure 4.22. The completed glazing along the side and rear wall

- **Pan** to the area shown in Figure 4.23.

- At the front of the building, draw the glazing for the top window and then use **MODIFY/ Array** with **1 column** and **2 rows**, and **2000** between the rows to create the lower pane.

The 2000 will either have a positive or negative value depending on where you start. Can you remember why? If not, refer to the previous methods. The partly completed glazing for the front of the building is shown in Figure 4.23.

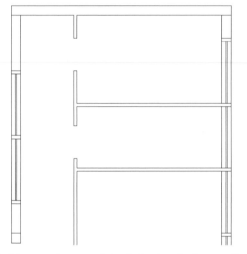

Figure 4.23. The partly completed glazing in the vertical front wall

- Use **MODIFY/Offset** to copy the main door reveal line to the left by 100mm to form the window mullion to the left of the main door, as shown in Figure 4.24.

- Draw the glazing in the front wall, as shown in Figure 4.24.

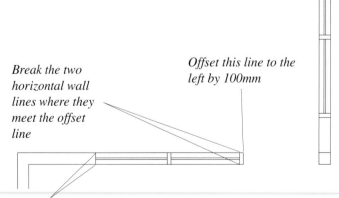

Break the two horizontal wall lines where they meet the offset line

Offset this line to the left by 100mm

Break the two horizontal wall lines at the window reveal

Figure 4.24. The partly completed glazing in the horizontal front wall

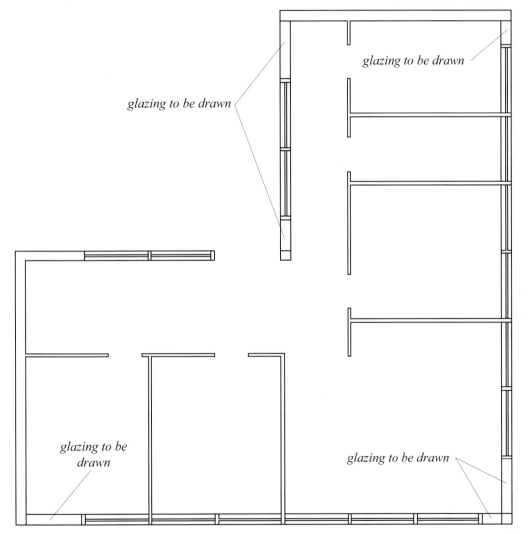

■ Use **MODIFY/Break** to break the two horizontal wall lines at the junction of the new line which has just been created by offseting by 100mm, as shown in Figure 4.24.

■ Use **MODIFY/Break** to break the two horizontal wall lines at the junction of the window reveal, as shown in Figure 4.24. Both of these breaks are in preparation for converting to 3D in Chapter 9.

Figure 4.25 shows the almost completed glazing. We still have to draw the odd-sized glazing in the building where it adjoins the corners.

glazing to be drawn

glazing to be drawn

glazing to be drawn

glazing to be drawn

Figure 4.25. *The building showing the remaining glazing to be drawn*

■ **Pan** and **Zoom** if necessary to the area shown in Figure 4.26.

Using the same method as before, we will draw a central line, **Offset** and then **Erase** it. This time we will introduce a different Osnap: **Perpendicular**, as shown in Figure 4.26.

■ Use **DRAW/Line** and the command line will prompt

Command: _line Specify first point: *_mid of (Choose mullion, as shown in Figure 4.26)*

Specify next point or [Undo]:   *_per to (Choose inner wall, as shown in Figure 4.26)*

Specify next point or [Undo]:   **Enter**

Why do you think that we have used **Perpendicular** to the second line rather than using **Midpoint** again? Try **Midpoint** and you will see.

■ **MODIFY/Offset** the line by 20mm above and below.

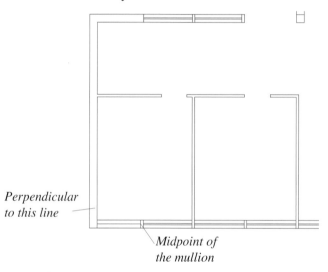

Perpendicular to this line

Midpoint of the mullion

Figure 4.26. Drawing the odd sized windows

■ **MODIFY/Erase** the central line.

■ Repeat this for the remaining windows which adjoin a wall, so that the glazing is completed.

■ **Save** the drawing.

Next, we will complete the wall to the WC and draw in the doors throughout the building.

Chapter 5 – Drawing with Arcs

B efore drawing the doors with arcs, we will depict the double door to the WC as straight lines so that we can practise the **Mirror** command.

Copying with the Mirror Command

The **Mirror** command allows us to make a copy of an object about an axis. First we will draw the 600mm-long partition shown in Figure 5.1. Then we will draw an axis line and mirror the partition about it.

- Make the **Walls** layer **Current**.

- Ensure that **Snap** is **On** and **Osnap** is **Off**.

- Use **DRAW/Line** to draw the 100mm-wide partition 600mm long, as shown in Figure 5.1.

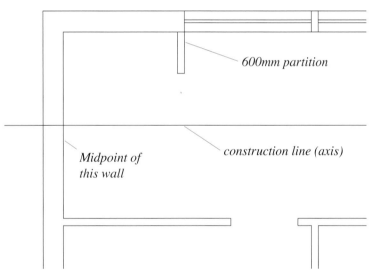

Figure 5.1. The construction line from the Midpoint of the wall and the drawn partition

- Turn **Ortho** on by clicking on the **Ortho** button, as shown in Figure 5.2. This will allow only horizontal or vertical lines.

Figure 5.2. The Status bar

We will draw a **Construction Line** from the **Midpoint** of the wall, as shown in Figure 5.1. This line is the axis we will use for the **Mirror** command, and will be erased later.

*Remember that the line can be drawn only horizontally or vertically, because **Ortho** is on.*

- Use **DRAW/Construction Line** and the command line will prompt

> Command: _xline Specify a point or [Hor/Ver/Ang/Bisect/Offset]: _mid of **(Pick inner wall line as shown in Figure 5.1)**
>
> Specify through point: **(Draw the line horizontally)**
>
> Specify through point: **Enter**

- Pick **MODIFY/Mirror** and the command line will prompt

> Command: _mirror
>
> Select objects: 3 found   **(Pick by window or individually, as shown in Figure 5.3)**
>
> Select objects: **Enter**
>
> Specify first point of mirror line: _   **int of (construction line and wall)**
>
> Specify second point of mirror   **_nea to (Pick anywhere on the construction line)**
>
> Delete source objects? [Yes/No] <N>:   **Enter**

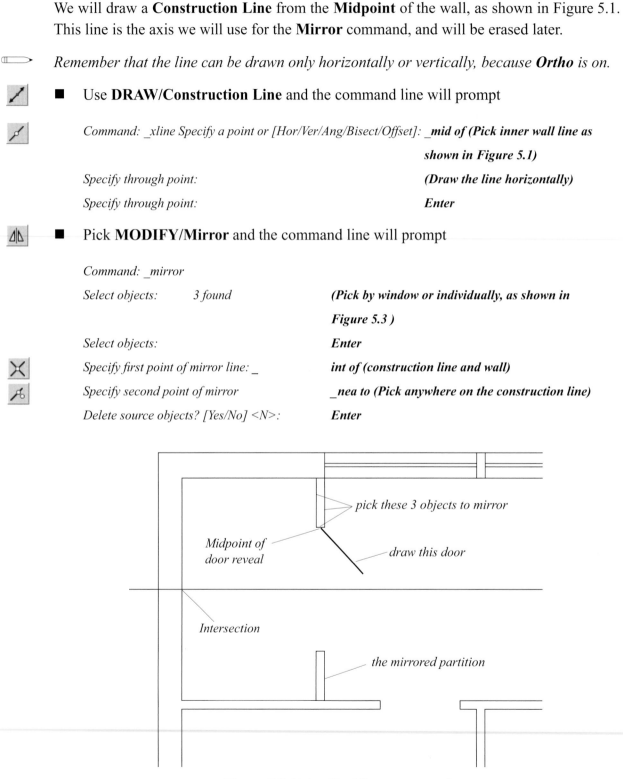

Figure 5.3. Using the Mirror command

- Make **Doors** the **Current** layer in readiness for drawing the doors.

- Turn **Snap Off**.

- Turn **Ortho Off**.

- Use **DRAW/Line** to draw in one of the doors from the **Midpoint** of the door reveal, 750mm long and at an angle of **315°**, as shown in Figure 5.3.

    Command: _line Specify first point: **(Pick the Midpoint of the door reveal)**

    Specify next point or [Undo]:   **@750<315 Enter (draws a line 750mm long at an angle of 315°)**

    Specify next point or [Undo]:   **Enter**

- Use **MODIFY/Mirror** again to mirror the door to the other side of the reveal, as shown in Figure 5.4.

- **MODIFY/Erase** the construction line.

- Ensure that **Snap** is **On**.

- **MODIFY/Break** the junctions between the new 600mm partitions and the previously drawn walls, as shown in Figure 5.4.

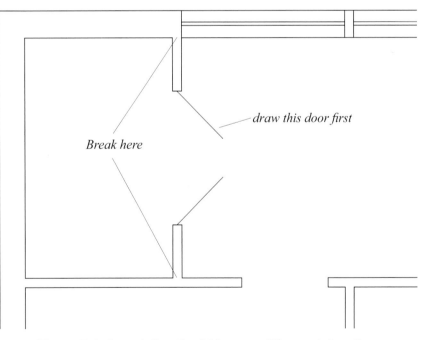

Figure 5.4. Completing the 600mm partition and door lines

Drawing Arcs

In AutoCAD, arcs must always be drawn **anticlockwise**, so the sequence of picking objects is crucial. We will use two different methods of drawing the arcs. In the first method we will specify the start point, the centre of the arc and the included angle. In the second method we will specify the start and end points and the radius of the arc. You will notice that we do not use the **Arc** button, as it only offers the default option of three points – a start, a second point on the arc and an end.

- Ensure that the **Doors** layer is **Current**.

- From the **DRAW/Arc** pull-down menu select **Start, Center, Angle** and the command line will prompt

    Command: _arc Specify start point of arc or [Center]:   **_end of (Select, as shown in Fig. 5.5)**

    Specify second point of arc or [CEnter/ENd]:   *_c*

    Specify center point of arc: **_end of (Select, as shown in Fig. 5.5)**

    Specify end point of arc or [Angle/chord Length]:   *_a Specify included angle:* **90**   ***Enter***

- Use **DRAW/Line** to draw in the door line from the **Endpoint** of the reveal to the **Endpoint** of the **Arc** to complete the doorway, as shown in Figure 5.5.

As Figure 5.6 shows, the second doorway is scribed in the same way. However, we will use a different **Arc** option – **Start**, **End** and **Radius**. To use this we must draw the door line first.

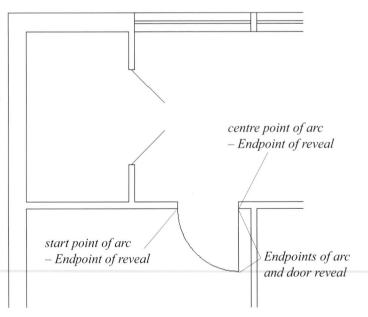

centre point of arc – Endpoint of reveal

start point of arc – Endpoint of reveal

Endpoints of arc and door reveal

Figure 5.5. *Drawing the doors with arcs and lines*

- Use **DRAW/Line** to draw in the door line from the **Endpoint** of the reveal 1000mm long, as shown in Figure 5.6.

- From the **DRAW/Arc** pull-down menu select **Start, End, Radius** and the command line will prompt

  Command: _arc Specify start point of arc or [CEnter]:   **_end of (Pick as shown in Figure 5.6)**

  Specify second point of arc or [CEnter/ENd]:   _e

  Specify end point of arc: **_end of (Pick as shown in Figure 5.6)**

  Specify center point of arc or [Angle/Direction/Radius]: _r Specify radius of arc: **1000**   **Enter**

- Complete the doors, as shown in Figure 5.7 with the **Line** and **Arc** commands using either of the two methods shown above. All doors have a radius of 1000mm.

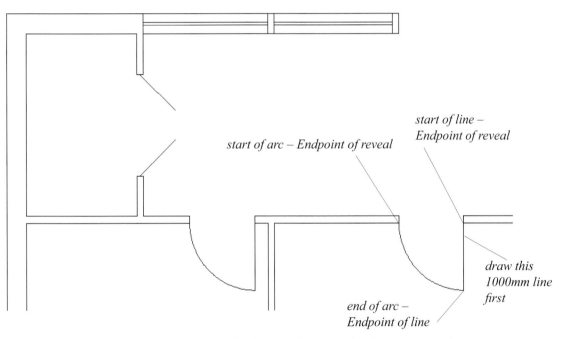

Figure 5.6. Drawing the door swing with the Arc command

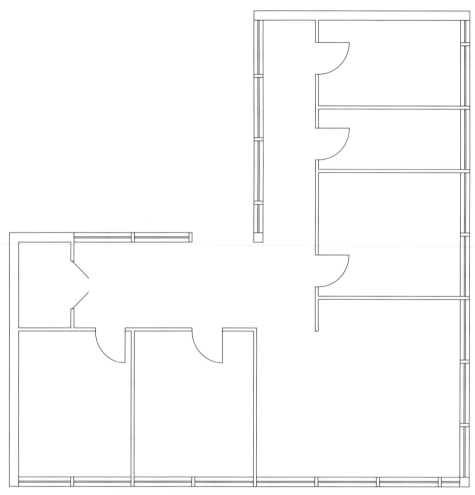

Figure 5.7. The completed doors

To draw the front double door, as shown in Figure 5.8, we will use the **Arc** command again using the **Start**, **End**, **Angle** option. In addition we will use the new **Object Snap** tool to find the **midpoint between two objects** where the door arcs will meet at the centre of the doorway, as shown in Figure 5.8.

- Ensure that **Osnap** is turned **On** and **Snap** is **Off.**

- **Use DRAW/Line** to draw in both door lines 1000mm long, as shown in Figure 5.8.

- To draw the first arc use **DRAW/Arc/Start**, **End**, **Angle** from the pull-down menu and the command line will prompt

  Command: _arc Specify start point of arc or [Center]:   **(Pick the Endpoint, as shown in Figure 5.8)**
  Specify second point of arc or [Center/End]: _e   **(Hold the Shift key down and right-click)**

- The **Object Snap** floating menu will appear. Click on **Mid Between 2 Points**

  Specify end point of arc: _m2p First point of mid: **(Click on left side of the door, as shown in Fig. 5.8)**
  Second point of mid: _a   **(Click on right side of the door, as shown in Fig.5.8)**
  Specify center point of arc or [Angle/Direction/Radius]: ***a***   ***Enter***
  Specify included angle: ***90***   ***Enter***

- Use **DRAW/Arc/Start**, **End**, **Angle** to complete the second arc as shown in Figure 5.8.

- **Save** the drawing.

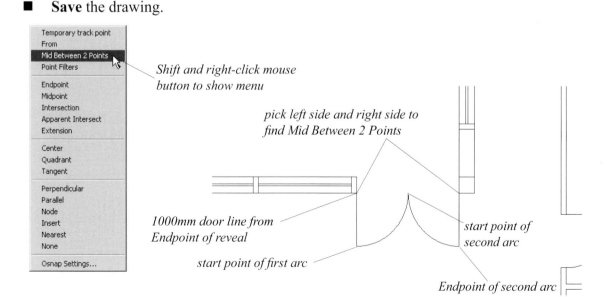

Figure 5.8. Drawing the front double door with the Start, End, Angle option of Arc and Mid Between 2 Points Object Snap

Chapter 6 – Making Reusable Symbols

If you plan to reuse a symbol you have drawn in AutoCAD, you can create a **Block**. When a **Block** is made, AutoCAD assembles the separate objects in the original symbol to form one object.

When a **Block** is inserted into a drawing, it can be resized, stretched and rotated. Because these symbols can also be used in other drawings, they need be drawn only once.

Rules for Drawing Blocks

Blocks drawn on **Layer 0** have a special adaptive quality. When a **Block** that consists of objects drawn on **Layer 0** is inserted into another layer, it assumes the colour and linetype of that layer. The current layer's properties override any colour or linetype assigned to that **Block**. If you draw a **Block** on any layer other than **Layer 0**, it will retain the colour and linetype assigned to it.

A **Block** must also have an insertion point. This is a reference basepoint to which the **Block** is related and which you will use to position the **Block** when it is inserted into the drawing. When the **Block** is inserted into the drawing the cursor will be shown at the insertion point for that **Block**.

Exporting Blocks

One way to export blocks into other drawings is with the **WBlock** command. This sequence is described on page 78.

Creating Blocks for the Drawing

We will now create **Blocks** of the furniture symbols to be inserted in the drawing, all of which are shown in Figure 6.18. We will practise new commands whilst creating each shape and then create the **Blocks** after completing all of the drawings, although in practice you can create **Blocks** directly after drawing each object.

- Make layer **0** the **Current** layer.

- Ensure that **Grid** and **Snap** are on.

- **Pan** to a clear area of the drawing where the grid is in view and unobstructed.

The Filing Cabinet

- Use **DRAW/Line** to draw the Filing Cabinet to the dimensions shown in Figure 6.1.

Figure 6.1. The Filing Cabinet Block

The Low Table

- Use **DRAW/Line** to draw the Low Table to the dimensions shown in Figure 6.2.

- To create the rounded corners on the Low Table we must firstly set the **Fillet Radius** value. Pick the **MODIFY/Fillet** button and the command line will prompt

Command: _fillet		
Current settings: Mode = TRIM, Radius = 0.000		
Select first object or [Polyline/Radius/Trim/mUltiple]:	**r (for radius)**	**Enter**
Specify fillet radius <0.000>:	**100**	**Enter**
Select first object or [Polyline/Radius/Trim/mUltiple]:	**(Pick a line)**	
Select second object	**(Pick an adjoining line)**	

The corner is changed to a filletted corner with a radius of 100 as shown in Figure 6.2.

- Reactivate the command by pressing the **Spacebar** and the command line will prompt

Command: FILLET	
Current settings: Mode = TRIM, Radius = 100.00	
Select first object or [Polyline/Radius/Trim/mUltiple]:	**(Pick one line)**
Select second object:	**(Pick an adjoining line)**

- Repeat this for the other two corners. The table should now have filletted corners, as shown in Figure 6.2.

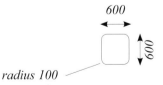

Figure 6.2. The Low Table with rounded corners using the Fillet command

THE COLLEGE OF WEST AND

The General Desk

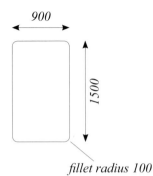

900

1500

fillet radius 100

Figure 6.3. *The General Desk with Filletted corners*

■ Use **DRAW/Line** and **MODIFY/Fillet** to draw the General Desk with the dimensions shown in Figure 6.3.

The General Chair

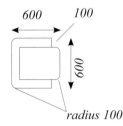

600 *100*

600

radius 100

Figure 6.4. *The General Chair with Filletted corners*

■ Use **DRAW/Line** and **MODIFY/Fillet** to draw the General Chair with the dimensions shown in Figure 6.4.

The Large Desk

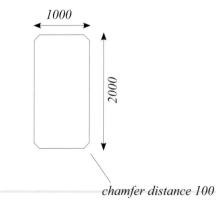

1000

2000

chamfer distance 100

Figure 6.5. *The Large Desk with Chamfered corners*

- Use **DRAW/Line** to draw the Large Desk as a rectangle shape to the dimensions shown in Figure 6.5.

To create the chamfered corners we must first set the chamfer distance values.

- Pick the **MODIFY/Chamfer** button and the command line will prompt

Command: _chamfer

(TRIM mode) Current chamfer Dist1 = 0.000, Dist2 = 0.000

Select first line or [Polyline/Distance/Angle/Trim/Method/mUltiple]:	***d***	***Enter***
Specify first chamfer distance <0.000>:	***100***	***Enter***
Specify second chamfer distance <100.000>:		***Enter***
Select first line or [Polyline/Distance/Angle/Trim/Method/mUltiple]:		***(Pick a line)***
Select second line:		***(Pick an adjoining line)***

- Reactivate the command by pressing the **Spacebar** and the command line will prompt

Command: CHAMFER

(TRIM mode) Current chamfer Dist1 = 100.000, Dist2 = 100.000

Select first line or [Polyline/Distance/Angle/Trim/Method/mUltiple]:	***(Pick a line)***
Select second line:	***(Pick an adjoining line)***

Repeat this for the other two corners. The Large Desk should now have chamfered corners, as shown in Figure 6.5.

*An alternative to pressing the **Spacebar** to reactivate the **Chamfer** command is to use the **mUltiple** option by entering **U** at the command line (whilst in the **Chamfer** command) which allows you to continue selecting objects to chamfer.*

The Low Chair

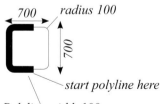

Figure 6.6. The Low Chair with Polyline

- Use **DRAW/Line** to draw the 'seat' (a 700x700 square) of the Low Chair to the dimensions shown in Figure 6.6.

To draw the chair back with a thick line we need to use a **Polyline**. A **Polyline** is a connected sequence of line or arc segments, created as a single object with a line width.

■ Pick **DRAW/Polyline** and the command line will prompt

> *Command: _pline*
>
> *Specify start point:*   **(Pick the start point on the chair seat, as shown in Figure 6.6)**
>
> *Current line-width is 0.000*
>
> *Specify next point or [Arc/Halfwidth/Length/Undo/Width]:*   **w (for width)**   **Enter**
>
> *Specify starting width <0.000>:*   **100**   **Enter**
>
> *Specify ending width <100.0000>:*   **Enter**
>
> *Specify next point or [Arc/Close/Halfwidth/Length/Undo/Width]:* **(Pick rear seat corner)**
>
> *Specify next point or [Arc/Close/Halfwidth/Length/Undo/Width]:* **(Pick other rear seat corner)**
>
> *Specify next point or [Arc/Close/Halfwidth/Length/Undo/Width]:* **(Pick end of arm)**
>
> *Specify next point or [Arc/Close/Halfwidth/Length/Undo/Width]:* **Enter**

■ Ensure that **Snap** is **Off**.

*Remember that the **Polyline** is a single object even though it has more than one segment.*

■ Use **MODIFY/Fillet** to fillet the rear corners of the **Polyline**

> *Command: _fillet*
>
> *Current settings: Mode = TRIM, Radius = 100.000*
>
> *Select first object or [Polyline/Radius/Trim/mUltiple]:*   **p (for polyline)**   **Enter**
>
> *Select 2D polyline:*   **(Pick the edge of the polyline)**
>
> *2 lines were filleted*

*If you have many corners to Fillet then use the **mUltiple** option, by entering **U** at the command line (whilst in the **Fillet** command), which allows you to continue selecting objects to fillet.*

Place the pickbox half on and half off the edge of the polyline to pick it.

Remember that filleting a polyline does not require you to pick two adjoining lines.

■ **MODIFY/Fillet** the front corners of the chair seat. The Low Chair should now be the same as shown in Figure 6.6.

The Sofa

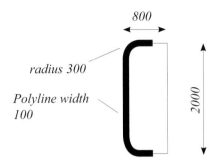

Figure 6.7. The Sofa created with Lines, Polyline and Filletting

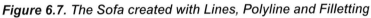

SNAP ■ Ensure that **Snap** is **On** to draw the sofa outline to the dimensions shown in Figure 6.7.

SNAP ■ Turn **Snap** off.

☐ ■ **MODIFY/Fillet** the sofa seat lines before filletting the polyline.

✏ *If **Snap** was set to **On** it could prevent selection of the polyline to fillet. To select a polyline, place the cursor on the polyline edge (half on, half off).*

The Director's Desk

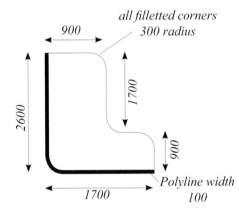

Figure 6.8. The Director's Desk

SNAP ■ Turn **Snap** on.

■ Construct the Director's Desk following the same process. The **Fillet/Radius** value is 300mm, as shown in Figure 6.8.

☐ ■ **MODIFY/Fillet** the lines before filletting the polyline.

The Operator's Chair

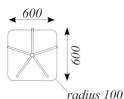

600

600

radius 100

Figure 6.9. The completed Operator's Chair

SNAP ■ Ensure that **Snap** is **On.**

■ Use **DRAW/Line** to draw the square outline of the Operator's Chair to the dimensions shown in Figure 6.9.

To construct the chair plinth we will use the **MODIFY/Polar Array** option to copy the legs around the central chair stem, depicted here with a circle set in the centre of the square.

■ Use **DRAW/Line** to draw two diagonal lines, as shown in Figure 6.10.

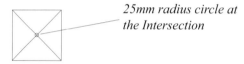

25mm radius circle at the Intersection

Figure 6.10. The two diagonal construction lines and the circle

⊘ ■ Use **DRAW/Circle** command and the command line will prompt

Command: _circle Specify center point for circle or [3P/2P/Ttr (tan tan radius)]:

╳   *_int of **(Pick Intersection of the diagonals)***

Specify radius of circle or [Diameter]:   **25**   **Enter**

■ **Erase** the two diagonal construction lines.

SNAP ■ Turn **Snap** off.

We will now draw the chair legs by using the **Polyline** command to draw one leg placed at the 12 o'clock **Quadrant** of the 25mm circle, as shown in Figure 6.11.

*You will probably need to **Zoom/Window** to the area just larger than the Chair.*

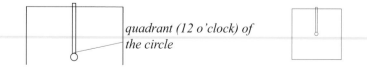

quadrant (12 o'clock) of the circle

Figure 6.11. The Chair leg drawn with a Polyline at the Quadrant of the Circle

■ Pick **DRAW**/**Polyline** and the command line will prompt

Command: _pline

From point: **_qua of (Pick the 12 o'clock position on the circle)**

Current line-width is 100.000

Specify next point or [Arc/Halfwidth/Length/Undo/Width]:   **w (for width)**   **Enter**

Starting width <100.000>:   **0**   **Enter**

Ending width <0.000>:   **Enter**

Specify next point or [Arc/Halfwidth/Length/Undo/Width]:   **@12.5<180**   **Enter**

Specify next point or [Arc/Close/Halfwidth/Length/Undo/Width]:   **@300<90 (leg length) Enter**

Specify next point or [Arc/Close/Halfwidth/Length/Undo/Width]:   **@25<0 (leg width)**   **Enter**

Specify next point or [Arc/Close/Halfwidth/Length/Undo/Width]:   **@300<270**   **Enter**

Specify next point or [Arc/Close/Halfwidth/Length/Undo/Width]:   **c (for close)**   **Enter**

We can now copy the chair leg with the **MODIFY**/**Array**/**Polar** command to place five legs around the central shaft, with the **Centre** of the **Polar** array being the **Centre** of the circle.

*Why did we draw the chair leg with a **Polyline**? To make it easier to pick when we **Array** it – remember that **Polylines** are one object so with a single pick all of the chair leg segments can be chosen.*

■ Use **MODIFY**/**Array** and the **Array** dialogue box will appear, as shown in Figure 6.12.

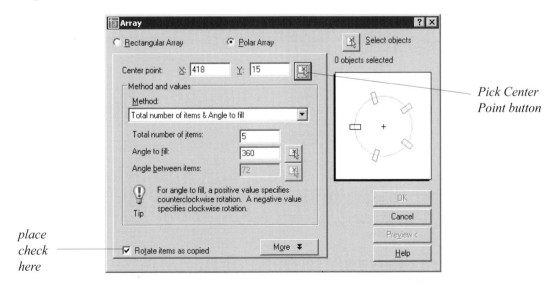

Figure 6.12. The Array dialogue box with Polar Array selected

- Click on the **Polar Array** radio button.

- Enter the **Total number of items** as **5**, as shown in Figure 6.12.

- Ensure that the **Angle to fill** is set to **360°**, as shown in Figure 6.12.

- Ensure that there is a tick in the **Rotate items as copied** box, as shown in Figure 6.12.

- Click on the **Pick Center Point** button. The **Array** dialogue box will disappear and the Command line will show

    Command: _array

    Specify center point of array: *_cen of (**Pick the centre of the circle**)*

- The **Array** dialogue box will reappear. Click on **Select objects** to choose the items to be arrayed.

- The **Array** dialogue box will disappear and the Command line will show

    Command: _array

    Specify center point of array: *_cen of*

    Select objects: 1 found   **(Pick the leg)**

    Select objects: **Enter**

- The **Array** dialogue box will reappear. Click **OK** in the **Array** dialogue box and the chair legs are copied around the central pillar.

- **MODIFY/Fillet** the corners of the chair with a 100mm radius.

The WC

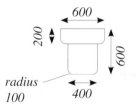

Figure 6.13. The WC with Filletted corners

- Turn **Snap** on.

- Use **DRAW/Line** to draw the WC to the dimensions shown in Figure 6.13.

- **MODIFY/Fillet** the corners, as shown in Figure 6.13.

The Wash Hand Basin

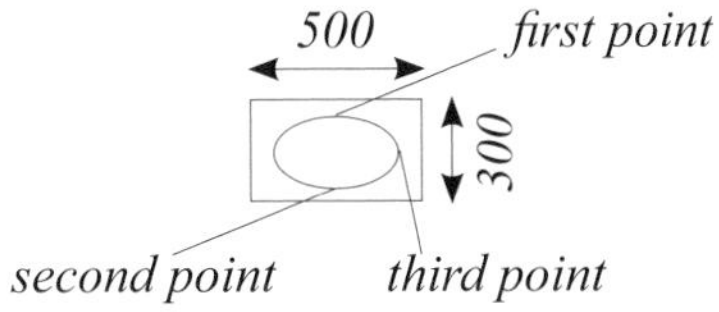

500   *first point*

300

second point   *third point*

Figure 6.14. The Wash Hand Basin drawn with the Ellipse command

- Use **DRAW/Line** to draw the outline of the Wash Hand Basin to the dimensions shown in Figure 6.14.

- Ensure that **Snap** is turned off.

- Turn **Ortho** on.

- Pick the **DRAW/Ellipse** command for the basin shape. The command line will prompt

Command: _ellipse

Specify axis endpoint of ellipse or [Arc/Center]:   **(Pick 1st point, as shown in Figure 6.14)**

Specify other endpoint of axis: **(Pick 2nd point, as shown in Figure 6.14)**

Specify distance to other axis or [Rotation]:   **(Pick 3rd point, as shown in Figure 6.14)**

The Planter

Figure 6.15. The Planter drawn with Polygon and Polyline

To draw the Planter we will first use the **Polygon** command to draw an **Inscribed** polygon (where the points of the sides would touch an imaginary circle drawn outside the polygon). We will then draw the plant with a freedrawn **Polyline**.

- Turn **Ortho** off.

- Pick **DRAW/Polygon** and the command line will prompt

Command: _polygon Enter number of sides <4>:   *5*   ***Enter***

Specify center of polygon or [Edge]:   ***(Pick a point)***

Enter an option [Inscribed in circle/Circumscribed about circle] <I>:   *i*   ***Enter***

Specify radius of circle: *450*   ***Enter***

- Use **DRAW/Polyline** to draw one leaf of the plant and use **MODIFY/Array** to array the leaves in a polar array. The Planter should be similar to Figure 6.15.

We are now ready to create **Blocks** of the symbols. We could, of course, have created a **Block** from each symbol directly after drawing it.

Creating Blocks of the Furniture Symbols

The names of the **Blocks** we are going to create are shown in Figure 6.18. Each insertion point is shown with an 'x'.

*It is usual to locate an **insertion point** somewhere on the block – the bottom left hand corner for example – but this will vary according to the type of block being created.*

*Where you see an **insertion point** just standing off the bottom left hand corner of a filletted or chamfered corner in Figure 6.18, it signifies the original corner before modifying to a fillet or chamfer. This is easily picked if you have created the blocks with **Snap On** as the cursor will jump to that point.*

Creating a Block

We have already done the first two of the steps for creating a **Block**:

- Ensure that the **Layer 0** is **Current**.

- Draw the objects which will compose the **Block**.

Follow these instructions for the **Low Table** symbol.

- From the **DRAW** toolbar select **Block/Make** and the **Block Definition** dialogue box will appear, as shown in Figure 6.16.

- Enter a **Block** name of up to 255 characters at the blinking cursor.

- Choose the **Block** insertion point with **Pick Point**. The dialogue box will disappear and the command line will prompt for an insertion point. Use the usual methods of selection; **Object Snap**, for example. The dialogue box will reappear.

- Press the **Select Objects** button. The dialogue box will disappear again. Select the objects to be made into the **Block** with the usual selection methods. Press **Enter** after the selection is completed. The dialogue box reappears.

- Click on **OK** and the **Block** is defined.

- Continue creating the remainder of the blocks as described above.

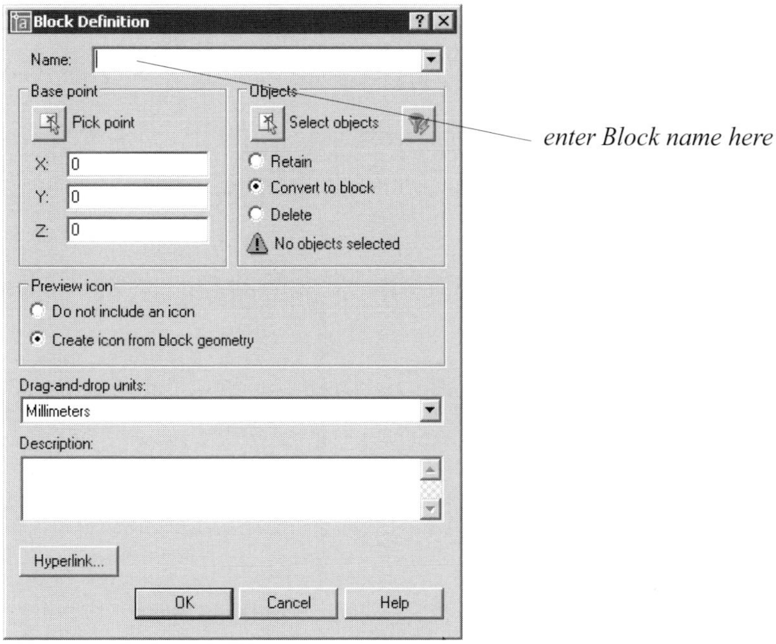

Figure 6.16. The Block Definition dialogue box

- Erase the symbols after making blocks – don't panic, as you have stored them permanently in the drawing.

Inserting the Blocks

- Make **Furniture** the **Current** layer. This is the destination layer for the blocks.

- Use **INSERT/Block** from the **Insert** pull-down menu and the **Insert** dialogue box will appear, as shown in Figure 6.17.

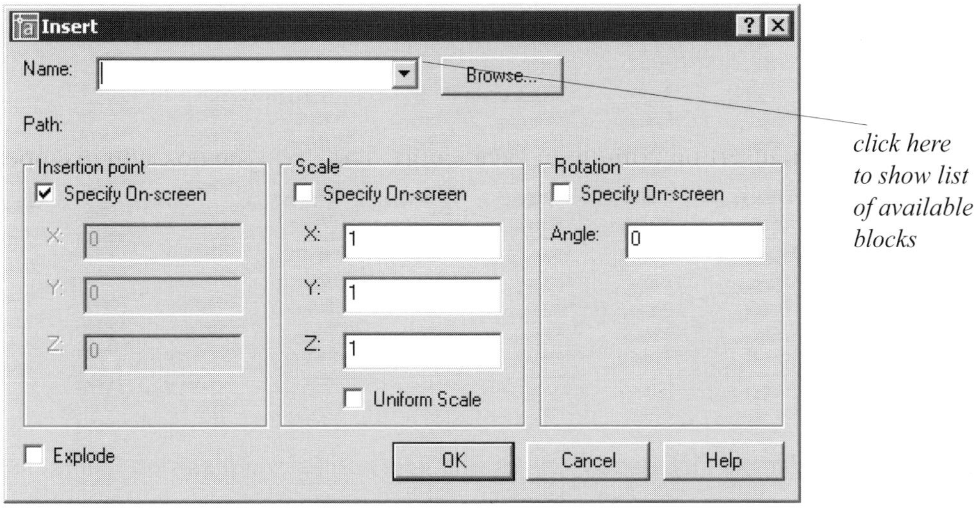

Figure 6.17. The Insert block dialogue box

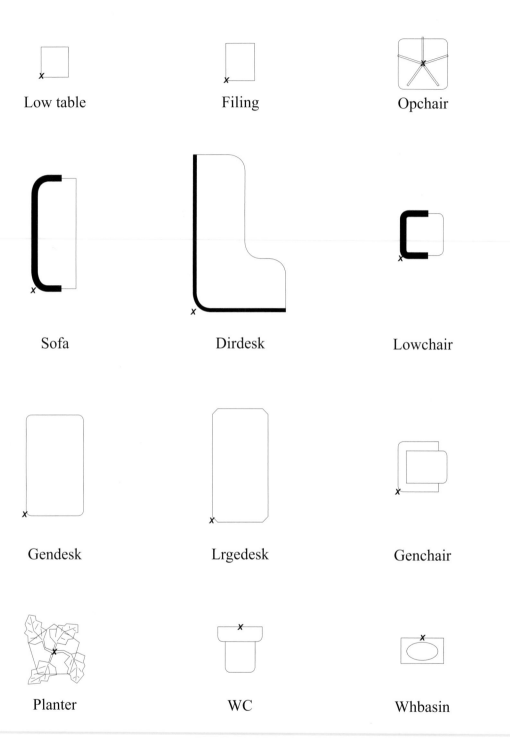

Low table

Filing

Opchair

Sofa

Dirdesk

Lowchair

Gendesk

Lrgedesk

Genchair

Planter

WC

Whbasin

Figure 6.18. Blocks included in the drawing with names and Insertion Points

■ Click on the **Name** drop-down menu and a listing of all the available **Blocks** will appear.

Your list of blocks in the pull-down menu should include all of the blocks just created.

■ Pick a **Block** name, as shown in Figure 6.19.

You will need to place a check in the 'Specify On-screen' box for the Rotation Angle of some of the Blocks, as shown in Figure 6.19, because they will not be inserted into the drawing at the same angle of rotation as they were drawn.

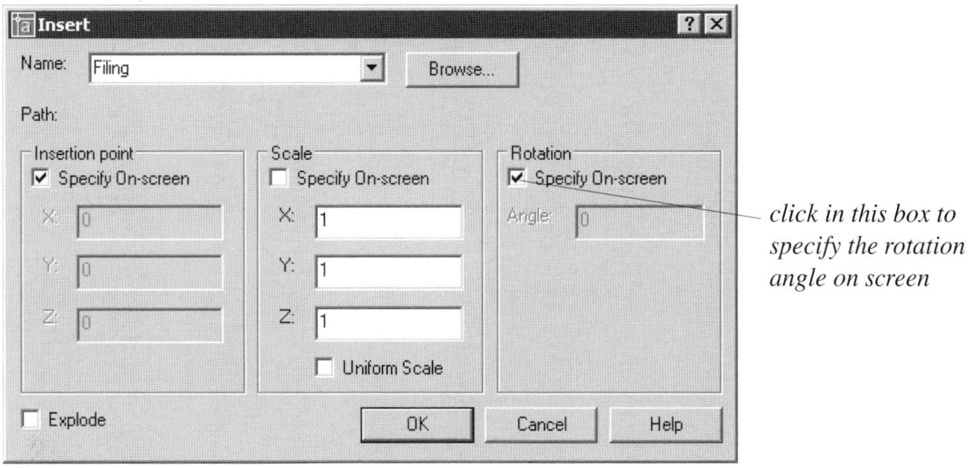

Figure 6.19. The Insert dialogue box showing the Filing block selected for insertion

■ Click on **OK**.

■ Insert the **Blocks**, as shown in Figure 6.20 or to your own design with blocks that you have created. (Read the steps below for some hints first.)

You will probably need to use MODIFY/Move and MODIFY/Rotate on some of the Blocks to locate them accurately.

■ When you **Insert** the **Opchair Block** around the circular table, use **DRAW/Circle** to draw a **Circle** of 1000mm radius and **MODIFY/Polar Array** the chairs around it using the **Centre** of the circle as the centre of the polar array.

■ To reduce the scale of the Planter, use **INSERT/Block** and the **Insert** dialogue box will appear, as shown in Figure 6.19.

■ Place a tick in the **Scale/Specify on screen** box.

■ Ensure the Planter is selected, and click on **OK**.

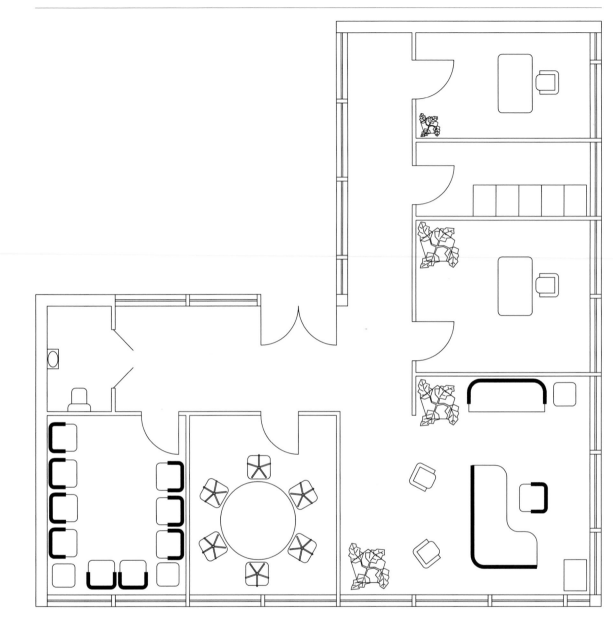

Figure 6.20. The furniture Blocks in their positions

■ The **Insert** dialogue box will disappear and the Command line will prompt

Command: _insert

Specify insertion point or [Scale/X/Y/Z/Rotate/PScale/PX/PY/PZ/PRotate]: **s (for scale)**   **Enter**

Specify scale factor for XYZ axes: **.5 (scales to half size)**   **Enter**

Specify insertion point: **(Pick a point in the drawing, with Osnap if necessary)**

■ When you have finished placing the **Blocks**, **Save** the drawing.

74

- Experiment by specifying **X** and **Y** instead of **S** for scale to obtain a different **Y scale factor** from the **X scale factor** with the other blocks to see the result.

*Use the **MODIFY/Copy** command to save time by copying a block you have inserted.*

*If you find that you have made a mistake in a block use the **MODIFY/Explode** command to convert the block back to its individual line objects. Redraw the block and make the block again with the same name. When AutoCAD asks if you want to redefine the block click **Yes**.*

Using the Tool Palettes to Insert Blocks

AutoCAD 2004 introduced tool palettes. This feature has been enhanced for AutoCAD 2005. A tool palette is a floating menu with tabs. The basic tool palette comprises a **Sample Office Project** tab, an **Imperial Hatches** tab, an **ISO Hatches** tab, and a **Command Tools** tab, as shown in Figure 6.21, but the exciting extra is that you can customise the tool palette to add a new tab with your own content. This is done in conjunction with the **Design Center**, which allows you (amongst other things) to open drawings by dragging from the **Design Center Tree** view into the drawing area, and to search for drawings and components.

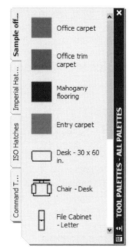

Figure 6.21. The standard tool palettes

We will create a new tab which contains all of the blocks previously created for the Furniture layer.

- Use **VIEW/Zoom/Extents**.

- Ensure that layer **Furniture** is the **Current** layer.

- Ensure that you have **Saved** the drawing after creating the blocks.

- If the Tool Palettes are not already displayed, click on the **Tool Palettes** icon in the **Standard** toolbar.

- Click on the **Design Center** icon and the **Design Center** palette will appear, as shown in Figure 6.22.

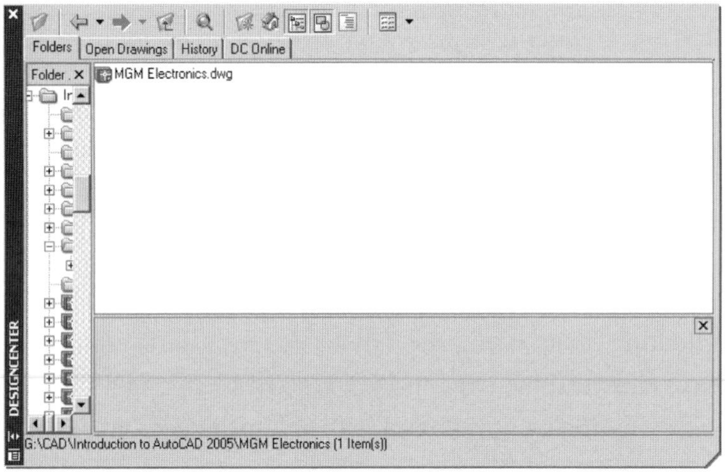

Figure 6.22. The Design Center palette showing the location of the MGM Electronics drawing file

- Locate the storage folder of your **MGM Electronics** drawing in the folder list on the left hand side of the palette. Its icon will appear in the right hand window, as shown in Figure 6.22.

- Right-click on the **MGM Electronics** icon and select **Create Tool Palette**, as shown in Figure 6.23.

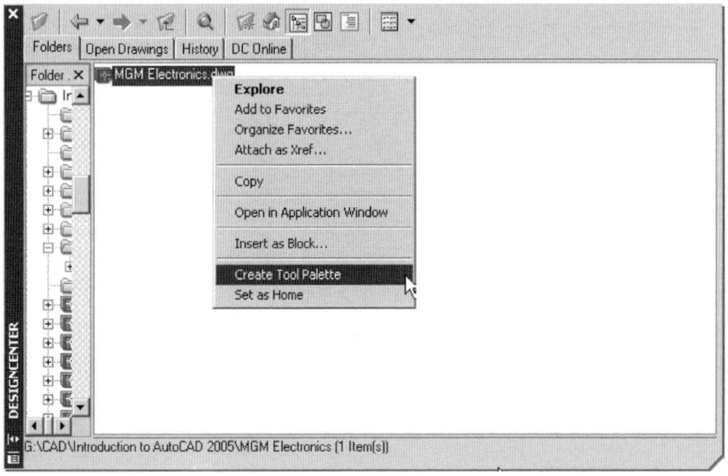

Figure 6.23. The Design Center palette

AutoCAD now searches the MGM Electronics drawing file to locate all the blocks created in that drawing. This will take a short time.

- A new tab will appear on the **Tool Palettes** called **MGM Electronics**, as shown in Figure 6.24.

Figure 6.24. The tool palette showing the added tool MGM Electronics, containing the blocks created in the drawing

- Close the **Design Center** palette by clicking on the **X** in the top left corner.

- Click on any of the blocks and then click on the drawing where you want to insert the block.

*When in the **Design Center**, if you choose a drawing file, the new tab will contain the blocks in the drawing as we have just done. If you create a new palette from a folder, the new tab shows all the drawings in the folder. Choosing a hatch pattern icon places all the hatch patterns from the hatch pattern file in the new tab.*

*Delete a **Tool Palette** by making the tab the active tab, right-click then pick **Delete Tool Palette**. To confirm the palette deletion, click **OK**.*

- **Save** the drawing.

To Export Blocks for Use in Other Drawings

■ To use Blocks created in our drawing in other drawings, type **wblock** at the command line

> *Command:* ***wblock***   ***Enter***

and the **Write Block** dialogue box appears, as shown in Figure 6.25.

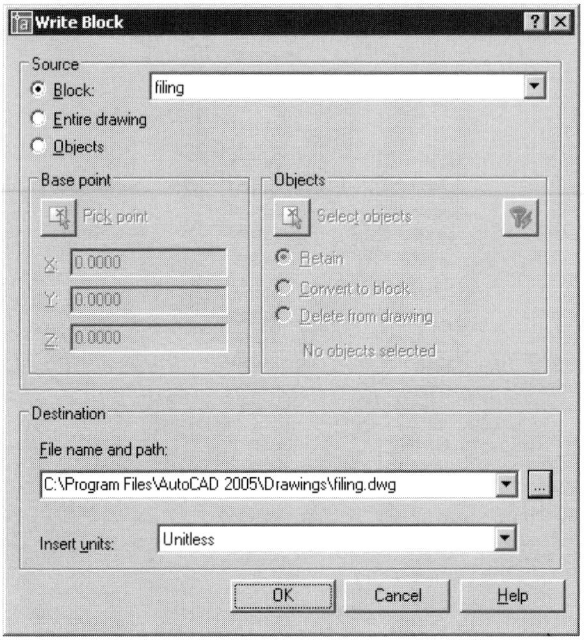

Figure 6.25. The Write Block dialogue box

■ Change the **Source** to **Block** and from the drop-down menu locate the block that you want to export.

■ Under the **Destination** section enter the name of the block (which could be different from the name of the original block) and change the path if necessary.

■ Click on **OK**.

The block is now exported, stored with a '.dwg' extension and can be used in any future drawings.

Chapter 7 – Drawing the Exterior Details

The exterior details include the boundary wall, patio, pond and driveway. We will draw these and use a hatch pattern to simulate the paviors on the patio area.

Drawing the Boundary Wall

We will now draw the 500mm-wide boundary wall with the **Multiline** command, which draws a double line and can cap the ends.

- Make **Boundary** the **Current** layer using the **Layer Properties Manager**.

- **Freeze** the **Furniture** and **Doors** layers.

- From the **FORMAT** pull-down menu choose **Multiline Style** and the **Multiline Styles** dialogue box will appear, as shown in Figure 7.1.

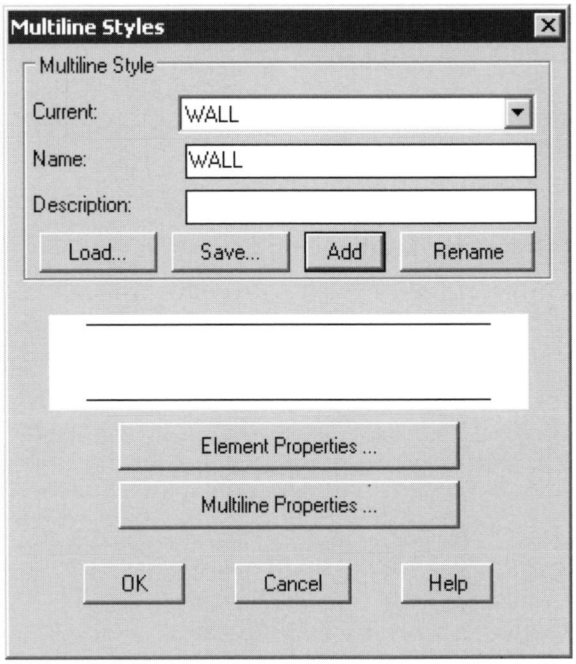

Figure 7.1. The Multiline Styles dialogue box with Wall as the Current style

- **Name** the new style '**WALL**' by overtyping the name **Standard** in the **Name** box.

- Click on **Add** to make it the **Current** style, as shown in Figure 7.1.

- To place caps at the end of the double line, click on **Multiline Properties**. The **Multiline Properties** dialogue box appears, as shown in Figure 7.2.

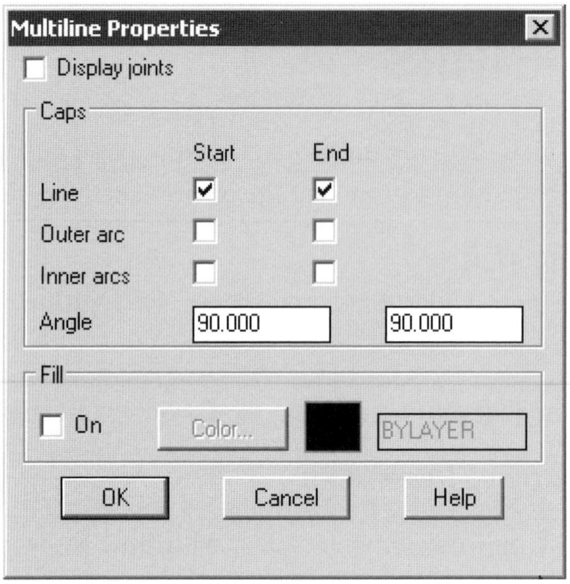

Figure 7.2. The Multiline Properties dialogue box with Caps at Start and End

- Put a check in the **Line Start** and **End** boxes.

- Click **OK**. The **Multiline Properties** dialogue box closes.

Note that the depiction of the style now has endcaps.

- Click **OK** in the **Multiline Styles** dialogue box.

- Use **VIEW/Zoom/All** to show the limits of the drawing.

To draw the boundary wall we will use absolute coordinates.

■   Pick **DRAW/Multiline** and the command line will prompt

Command: _mline

Current settings: Justification = Top, Scale = 20.00, Style = WALL

Specify start point or [Justification/Scale/STyle]:   **s (for scale)**   ***Enter***

Enter mline scale <20.00>:   **500 (sets the wall width to 500mm)**   ***Enter***

Current settings: Justification = Top, Scale = 500.00, Style = WALL

Specify start point or [Justification/Scale/STyle]:   **2000,24250**   ***Enter***

Specify next point: **28250,24250**   ***Enter***

Specify next point or [Undo]:   **28250,750**   ***Enter***

Specify next point or [Close/Undo]:   **1750,750**   ***Enter***

Specify next point or [Close/Undo]:   **1750,19000**   ***Enter***

Specify next point or [Close/Undo]:   ***Enter***

The drawing should now look like that shown in Figure 7.3.

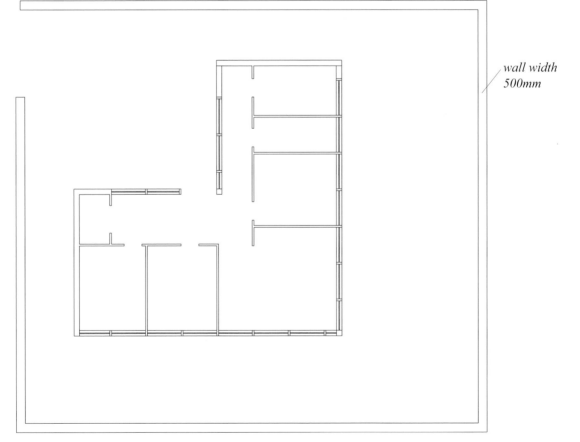

wall width 500mm

Figure 7.3. The completed Boundary Wall drawn with Multiline

*To make the wall more realistic, a height of approximately 500–750mm could be added to the wall as shown in Chapter 2, Figure 2.2. If you do this, remember that you must use the **MODIFY/Explode** command to create individual objects and the **Chprop** command to change the **Thickness** (which is what AutoCAD calls height).*

*Remember, also, that when using the **Thickness** command the top of the boundary wall will not appear solid until 3Dfaces have been applied. We use the **3DFace** command later in the book when the roof is constructed, so I suggest you gain the **3DFace** command skills on the roof first and return to the boundary wall later. (AutoCAD LT users should use the **Solid** command with **Fill** turned to **Off**).*

Drawing the Driveway

We can now draw the driveway at the entrance to the site using the **Arc/3Points** command. This command allows us to specify three points: a start, end and a third point on the arc.

- Create a layer called **Driveway** with a colour of your choice and make it the **Current** layer. Use **VIEW/Zoom/Window** to zoom to the area shown in Figure 7.4.

- From the **DRAW/Arc** pull-down menu pick **3 Points** and the command line will prompt

   *Command: _arc Specify start point of arc or [Center]:   **_endp of (Pick, as shown in Figure 7.4)***
   *Specify second point of arc or [Center/End]:   **(Pick, as shown in Figure 7.4)***
   *Specify end point of arc: **_endp of (Pick, as shown in Figure 7.4)***

- Repeat this for the second arc, as shown in Figure 7.4, using the **Start**, **End**, **Direction** option. Pick the **Nearest** Osnap for the first point, the **Endpoint** Osnap for the second and drag the arc into position for the **Direction**.

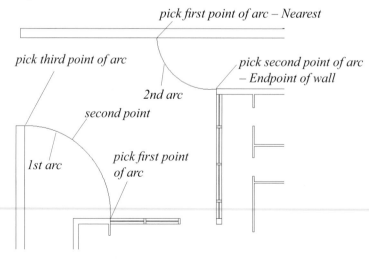

Figure 7.4. Using the Arc command to draw the driveway

Changing the Linetype

So far we have drawn with a continuous linestyle, which is the AutoCAD default style. We can, however, utilise the many different styles from the AutoCAD library. A linetype is a repeating pattern of dashes, dots and blank spaces displayed in a line or a curve. You assign linetypes to objects either by layer or by specifying the linetype explicitly, independent of layers.

We will draw a dashed linetype across the driveway to signify the end of a surface.

- Create a layer called **Drivewayedge** with a colour of your choice and make it the **Current** layer. With the **Layers Properties Manager** dialogue box still open, click on **Continuous** on the **Drivewayedge** layer.

- The **Select Linetype** dialogue box will appear, as shown in Figure 7.5. Click on **Load**.

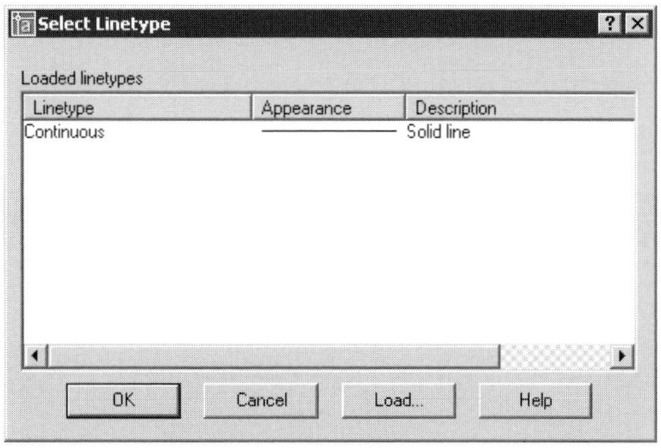

Figure 7.5. The Select Linetype dialogue box

- The **Load or Reload Linetypes** dialogue box will appear, as shown in Figure 7.6. Click on the first in the list: the **ISO dash** style. You will see a representation of what the style looks like next to its name.

- Click **OK**.

- The **Load or Reload Linetypes** dialogue box will disappear and the linestyle will appear in the **Select Linetype** dialogue box. Click on the newly loaded style and click **OK**.

- The **Select Linetype** dialogue box will disappear. In the **Layers Properties Manager** dialogue box you will see the linetype has been changed from the default **Continuous** style to your selection. Click **OK**. The **Layers Properties Manager** dialogue box will disappear.

We have now loaded a new linetype and assigned the style to the layer **Drivewayedge.**

Whatever we now draw on that layer, all the objects will be in the assigned linestyle.

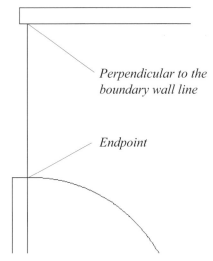

Figure 7.6. The Load or Reload Linetypes dialogue box

 ▪ Draw a line from the **Endpoint** of the boundary wall **Perpendicular** to the other boundary wall, as shown in Figure 7.7.

Perpendicular to the boundary wall line

Endpoint

Figure 7.7. The changed linetype still looks like a continuous linestyle until its linetype scale is changed

▪ Even though the line now looks as though it is solid, it is, in fact, a dashed line drawn at a scale of 1. To change the scale of the line (the size of the dashes and the spaces between them) click on the line. Blue squares called **Grips** will appear, one at either end and one in the middle, as shown in Figure 7.8.

▪ Use **MODIFY/Properties** and the **Properties Palette** will appear.

▪ Enter a **Linetype scale** of **5**, as shown in Figure 7.8.

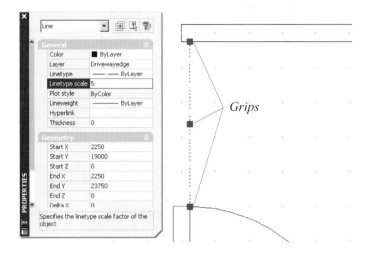

Figure 7.8. The dashed linestyle showing the blue grip boxes and the Properties palette and the linetype scale highlighted

■ Close the **Properties Palette** and press **Esc** on the keyboard to deselect the line. The linetype scale has now changed, as shown in Figure 7.10.

*We have changed the linetype scale of an individual object. AutoCAD has the facility to change the linetype scale globally: if we have multiple linetypes in the drawing we can change the scale of them all with one command rather than going through the process above. Use **FORMAT/Linetype**. In the **Linetype Manager** dialogue box, click on **Show Details** to expand the dialogue box and enter a new value for **Global scale factor**. Click on **OK**.*

Drawing a Point

A point in AutoCAD is an object which can be used as a marker. There are 20 different styles, as shown in Figure 7.9. We shall place a marker in the drawing to signify the future position for the exterior lighting column.

- ■ Create a layer called **Exterior Lighting** with a colour of your choice and make it the **Current** layer.

- ■ Use **FORMAT/Point Style** and the **Point Style** dialogue box will appear, as shown in Figure 7.9.

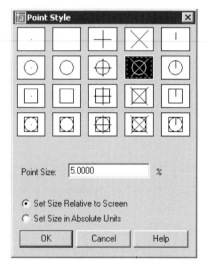

Figure 7.9. The Point Style dialogue box showing the 20 styles available

- ■ Click on any style and then click **OK**.

- ■ Use **DRAW/Point/Single Point** and place a point at the position shown in Figure 7.10.

Drawing a Revision Cloud

We will mark the position of the future lighting column with explanatory text surrounded by a **Revision Cloud**. A **Revision Cloud** is used to draw attention to some feature (usually a change in the drawing, hence its name) but here we are adding a note to show a later addition to the site.

- ■ Ensure that **Exterior Lighting** is the **Current** layer.

- ■ Use **VIEW/Zoom/Window** to display the area shown in Figure 7.11.

- ■ Use **DRAW/Revision Cloud**

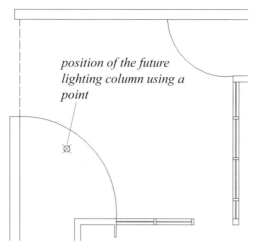

position of the future lighting column using a point

Figure 7.10. *The Point marker showing the position for the future lighting column*

Command: _revcloud

Minimum arc length: 15 Maximum arc length: 15 Style: Normal

Specify start point or [Arc length/Object/Style] <Object>:   **a (for arc)**   **Enter**

Specify minimum length of arc <15>:   **1000**   **Enter**

Specify maximum length of arc <1000>:   **Enter**

Specify start point or [Arc length/Object/Style] <Object>:   **(Pick a start point and**

Guide crosshairs along cloud path...   **move the mouse pointer**

Revision cloud finished.   **in a circle)**

■ Use **DRAW/Line** to draw a line from the **Revision Cloud** to the vicinity of the **Point** marker to indicate its position, as shown in Figure 7.11.

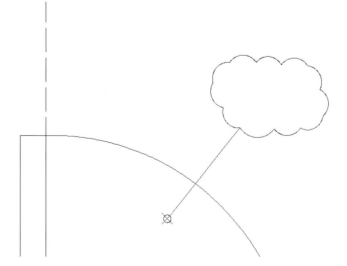

Figure 7.11. *The Revision Cloud with a line drawn to the Point object*

87

Adding Multiline Text

- Turn **Osnap** off.

- To add the text in the Revision Cloud use **DRAW/Text/Multiline Text** and the cursor will show the greyed out letters 'abc' indicating the current height and text style (probably very small). At the same time the command line asks for a first corner of the invisible bounding box around the text

> *Command: _mtext Current text style: "Standard" Text height: 2.5*
>
> *Specify first corner:* **(Pick a point in the Cloud)**
>
> *Specify opposite corner or [Height/Justify/Line spacing/Rotation/Style/Width]:*
>
> **(Pick a point diagonally opposite)**
>
> *Command:* **Enter**

- Type a text height and choose a font from the drop-down on the **Text Formatting** dialogue box, as shown in Figure 7.12.

- Enter the text, as shown in Figure 7.12.

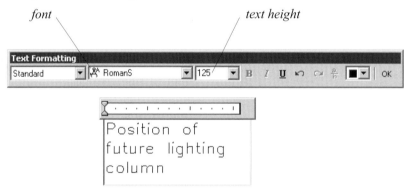

Figure 7.12. The Multiline Text Editor and Styles pull-down boxes

- Click your cursor anywhere outside the **Multiline Text Editor** and the box disappears leaving the text only, as shown in Figure 7.13.

If your text box is too small, AutoCAD automatically extends the box downwards as you are typing. The text automatically wraps at the right side.

*Use **MODIFY/Move** to reposition the text inside the Revision Cloud if it is not in a suitable position.*

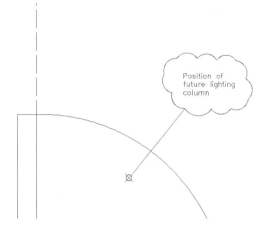

Figure 7.13. The completed Multiline Text inside the Revision Cloud

Drawing the Patio Edge

The edge of the patio can be drawn using a combination of **Polylines** and **Polyarcs**. Why are we going to use **Polyline** to do this? Because it will be easier to pick when we fill the area with a hatch pattern.

- Make **Patioedge** the **Current** layer.

- **Freeze** the layer **Exterior Lighting**.

- Use **VIEW/Zoom/Extents** to display the area shown in Figure 7.14.

- Turn **Osnap** on.

- Pick the **DRAW/Polyline** button and the command line will prompt

Command: *_pline*

Specify start point: *_int of* **(Pick the building, as shown in Figure 7.14)**

Current line-width is 0.000

Specify next point or [Arc/Halfwidth/Length/Undo/Width]:   **(Draw a short polyline as shown in Figure 7.14)**

Specify next point or [Arc/Close/Halfwidth/Length/Undo/Width]: a (for arc)   **Enter**

- Draw as many **Polylines** and **Polyline arcs** as you feel necessary to complete the edge of the patio in between the **Intersections** of the building corners.

Specify endpoint of arc or[Angle/CEnter/CLose/Direction/Halfwidth/Line/Radius/Second pt/Undo/Width]:

      _int of (Pick as in Figure 7.14)

■ Complete the pond outline with a combination of polylines and polyarcs, as shown in **Figure 7.14.**

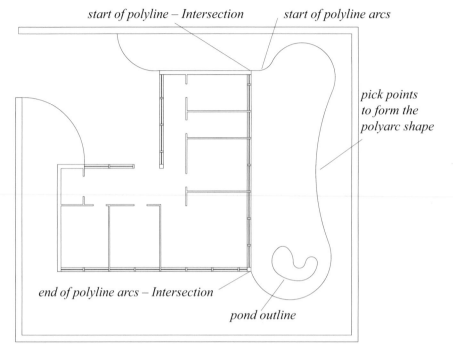

start of polyline – Intersection

start of polyline arcs

*pick points
to form the
polyarc shape*

end of polyline arcs – Intersection

pond outline

Figure 7.14. The patio and pond outline drawn with Polyline Arcs

Using a Hatch Pattern for the Patio

Hatching fills a specified area in a drawing with a pattern that is predefined or one that you can create. We will use a predefined pattern.

■ Make **PatioHatch** the **Current** layer.

■ Use **DRAW/Hatch** and the **Boundary Hatch and Fill** dialogue box will appear, as shown in Figure 7.15.

■ Click on the **Pattern** drop-down menu and select the **AR-Hbone** style, as shown in Figure 7.15.

■ Changing the **Scale** to anything between 10 and 20 will give a less dense pattern, but choose your own. A scale of value 1 would be usual.

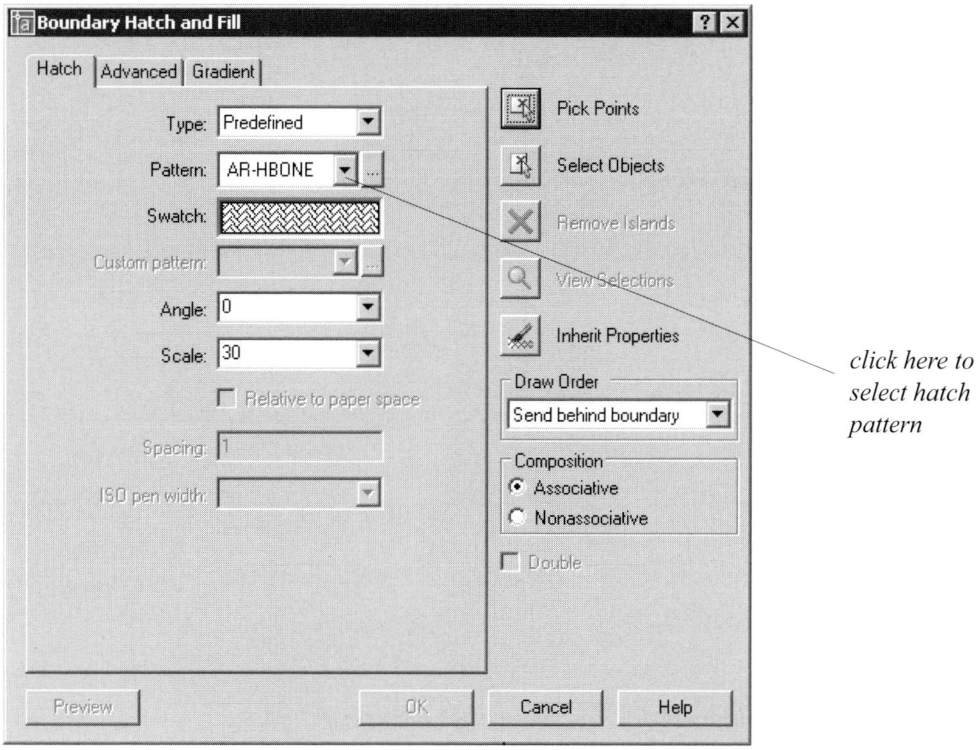

Figure 7.15. The Boundary Hatch dialogue box

■ Click on **Pick Points** and the dialogue box disappears and the command line will prompt

Command: _bhatch

Select internal point: Selecting everything...   **(Click within the patio boundary)**

Selecting everything visible...

Analyzing the selected data...

Analyzing internal islands...

Select internal point: **Enter**

*If clicking on **Pick Points** gives a '**Valid hatch boundary not found**' message, or seems to select almost everything in the drawing, use the **Select Objects** button to pick the patio outline, the building line and the pond outline. Remember that the building line is actually two separate lines (it was broken near the bottom). Ensure that both lines are selected, otherwise the hatch will show gaps in the pattern.*

The dialogue box reappears after you press **Enter**. You can now either look at the hatch pattern in situ with **Preview** or you can **OK** the pattern. **Preview** gives the opportunity to change the pattern and scale, for example, before finally clicking on **OK**.

Figure 7.16 shows the completed patio area after hatching.

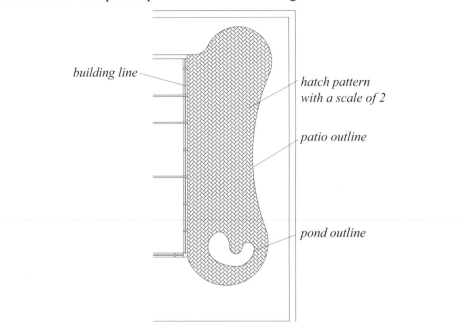

building line

hatch pattern with a scale of 2

patio outline

pond outline

Figure 7.16. The patio after being hatched

Calculating the Area of a Shape

At this point we can take the opportunity to practise finding the area of a shape. We will find the area of the patio; this would be very useful information for calculating the building cost. The only problem is that we have the pond outline to deduct from the overall area. Fortunately AutoCAD handles this very easily by incorporating **Add** and **Subtract** functions into the **Area** command. Lastly, we can also use the **Object** option to make one pick if the object to be measured is a closed boundary such as a circle, polyline, etc.

- Use **VIEW/Zoom/Window** to display the whole of the patio.

- Make layer **0 Current** and **Freeze** the layer **Patiohatch**.

- Load the **Inquiry** toolbar with **VIEW/Toolbars**.

*A quick alternative is to right-click with the mouse on any toolbar and click on **Inquiry** from the shortcut menu.*

The **Inquiry** toolbar will appear on screen.

■ Click on the **Area** button

> *Command: _area*
>
> | | | |
> |---|---|---|
> | *Specify first corner point or [Object/Add/Subtract]: a* | ***a (for add)*** | ***Enter*** |
> | *Specify first corner point or [Object/Subtract]: o* | ***o (for object)*** | ***Enter*** |
> | *(ADD mode) Select objects:* | ***(Pick the patio outline)*** | |
> | *Area = 112429265.60, Length = 34416.79* | | |
> | *Total area = 112429265.60* | ***(The area is displayed on the Command line)*** | |
> | *(ADD mode) Select objects:* | ***Enter*** | |
> | *Specify first corner point or [Object/Subtract]:* | ***s (for subtract)*** | ***Enter*** |
> | *Specify first corner point or [Object/Add]:* | ***o (for object)*** | ***Enter*** |
> | *(SUBTRACT mode) Select objects:* | ***(Pick the pond outline)*** | |
> | *Area = 6643157.34, Length = 13121.72* | | |
> | *Total area = 105786108.27* | ***(Final calculated area is displayed)*** | |
> | *(SUBTRACT mode) Select objects:* | ***Enter*** | |
> | *Specify first corner point or [Object/Add]:* | ***Enter*** | |

The total area is displayed in mm so the final area for the patio minus the pond is $105.78m^2$. Your final area will be different, of course, as your patio is a different shape and size.

*To calculate the area of an object which comprises joined lines use **Object Snaps** at the 'Specify first corner point' picking each line **Endpoint**.*

■ Use **INQUIRY/Area** to calculate the area of each of the rooms in the building.

■ Write down these areas as we will use them later.

■ Close the **Inquiry** toolbar.

■ **Save** the drawing.

Two-dimensional drawing is now complete. We can now start annotating the drawing with dimensions and text.

Chapter 8 – Dimensioning and Annotating the Drawing

Before dimensioning the drawing we need to set up the style and method of dimensioning through the **FORMAT**/**Dimension Styles** pull-down menu. We will save our own dimension style through the **Lines and Arrows**, **Text** and **Fit** tabs with values, as shown in Figure 8.1.

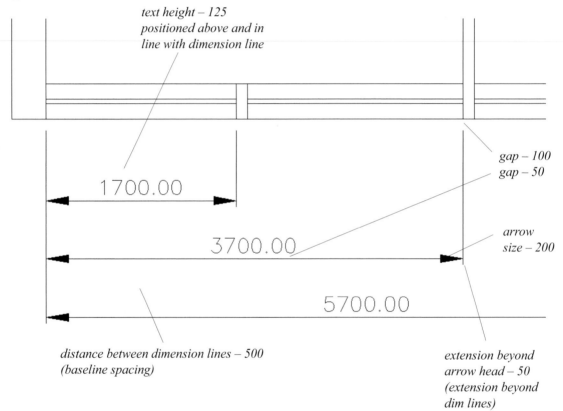

text height – 125
positioned above and in
line with dimension line

1700.00

3700.00

5700.00

gap – 100
gap – 50

arrow
size – 200

distance between dimension lines – 500
(baseline spacing)

extension beyond
arrow head – 50
(extension beyond
dim lines)

Figure 8.1. Dimension style details

Setting up the Dimension Style

■ Pick **FORMAT/Dimension Style** from the pull-down menu and the **Dimension Style Manager** dialogue box will appear, as shown in Figure 8.2.

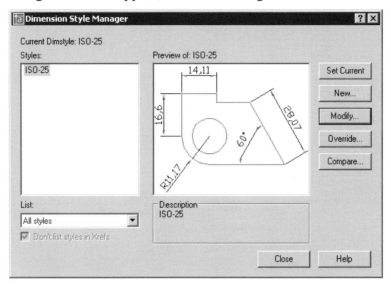

Figure 8.2. The Dimension Style Manager dialogue box

■ Pick the **Modify** button and in the **Lines and Arrows** tab enter the values highlighted in Figure 8.3. Don't worry what the preview looks like at this stage.

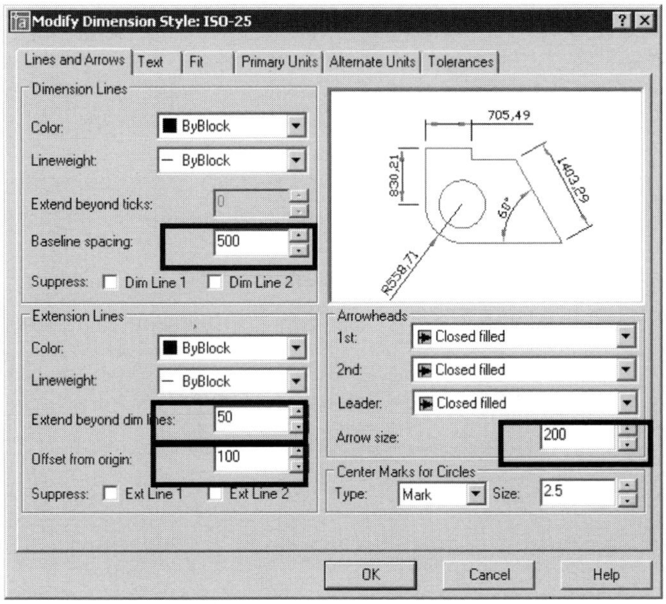

Figure 8.3. The Modify Dimension Style dialogue box – Lines and Arrows tab

■ Click on the **Text** tab and enter the values highlighted in Figure 8.4.

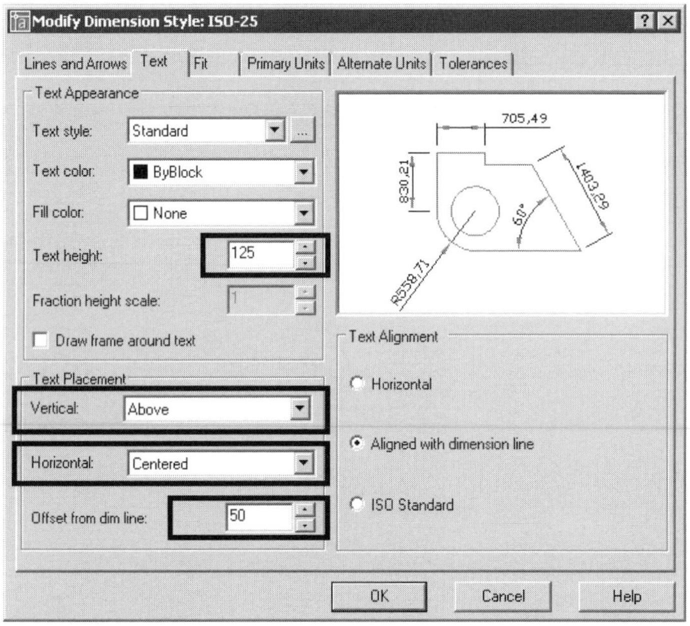

Figure 8.4. The Modify Dimension Style dialogue box – Text tab

■ Click on the **Fit** tab and select the options highlighted in Figure 8.5.

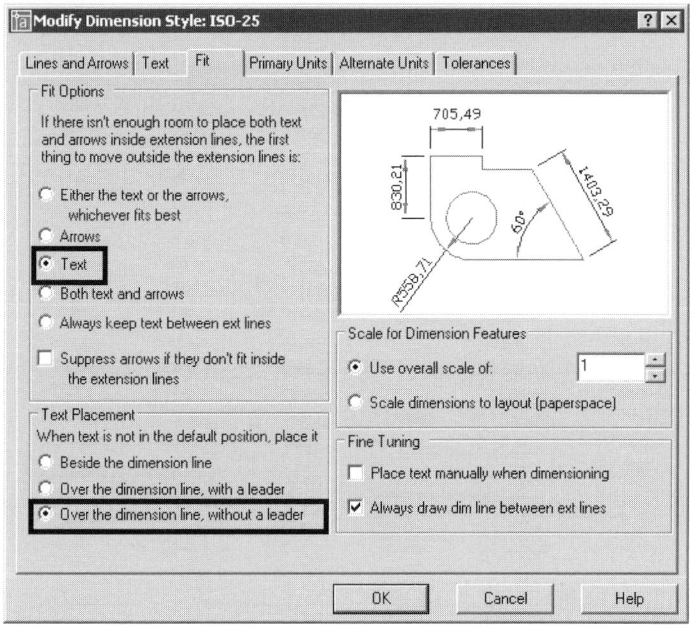

Figure 8.5. The Modify Dimension Style dialogue box – Fit tab

■ Click on the **Primary Units** tab and select the options highlighted in Figure 8.6.

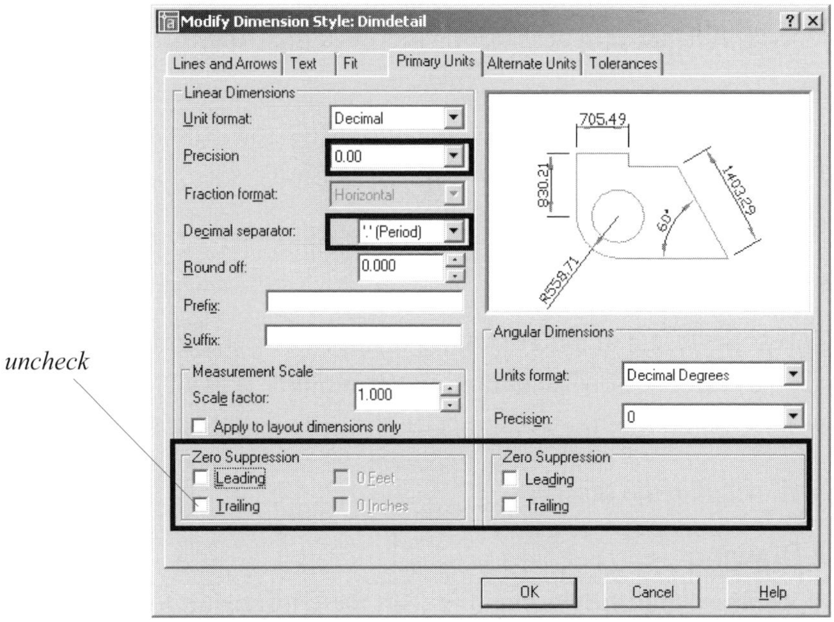

Figure 8.6. The Modify Dimension Style dialogue box – Primary Units tab

■ Click on **OK**. The **Dimension Style Manager** dialogue box reappears.

■ Save the new dimension style by clicking on **New**. The **Create New Dimension Style** dialogue box will appear, as shown in Figure 8.7.

■ Enter the **New Style Name** of **Dimdetail**.

■ Click on **Continue**.

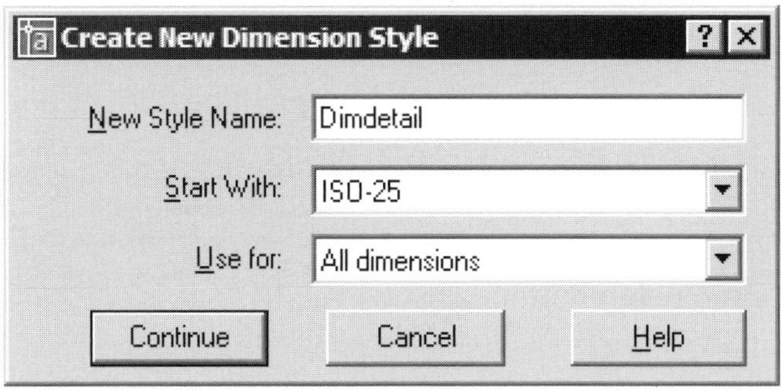

Figure 8.7. The Create New Dimension Style dialogue box

- The **New Dimension Style** dialogue box appears. Click **OK**.

The name of the new style will appear in the **Styles** window of the **Dimension Styles Manager** dialogue box.

- Click on the new name **Dimdetail**.

- Click on **Set Current**.

- Click on **Close**.

- Use **FORMAT/Text Style** and in the **Text Style** dialogue box ensure that you set the text height to zero. If the text height is set at a non-zero number it overrides any dimension text heights you have entered in the text tab. Click **Apply** and then click **Close**.

We are now ready to dimension the drawing.

Dimensioning the Drawing

- Pick the **VIEW/Toolbars** pull-down menu to load the **Dimension** toolbar, as shown in Figure 8.8. Position it conveniently on your screen.

Figure 8.8. The Dimension toolbar

- Make the **Dimensions** layer the **Current** layer.

- Ensure that the **Doors** layer is **Frozen.**

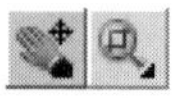

- **Pan** or **Zoom** to the bottom left corner of the building, as shown in Figure 8.9.

- Turn **Snap** on and off during dimensioning to pick the correct points. Osnaps can also be used.

Linear Dimensions

- Pick the **Linear Dimension** button.

> *Command: _dimlinear*
>
> *Specify first extension line origin or <select object>:*   ***Enter***
>
> *Select object to dimension:*   ***(Pick the 3700.00 internal window wall)***
>
> *Specify dimension line location or [Mtext/Text/Angle/Horizontal/Vertical/Rotated]:*
>
> ***(Drag the dimension to a suitable location)***
>
> *Dimension text = 3700.00*   ***(Click the left mouse button)***

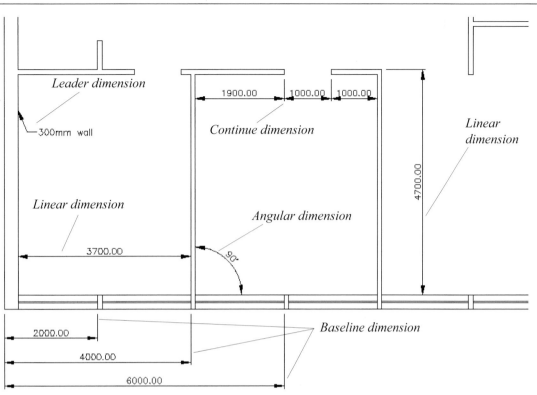

Figure 8.9. Dimensioning the drawing

■ Repeat the **Linear Dimension** for the **4700.00** dimension, as shown in Figure 8.9.

Baseline Dimensions

■ Now we will add the three dimensions in the bottom left of Figure 8.9. Pick the **Linear Dimension** button.

Command: _dimlinear

Specify first extension line origin or <select object>: **_endp of (Pick external corner)**

Specify second extension line origin: **_endp of (1st mullion line, as shown in Figure 8.9)**

Specify dimension line location or

[Mtext/Text/Angle/Horizontal/Vertical/Rotated]: **_endp of (1st mullion line)**

Dimension text = 2000.00 **(Drag the dimension to a suitable location and click)**

■ To create a baseline dimension pick the **Baseline Dimension** button and the command line will prompt you for another second point, using the first point chosen as the datum of the dimension.

Command: _dimbaseline

Specify a second extension line origin or [Undo/Select] <Select>:   **_endp of (2nd mullion line)**

Dimension text = 4000.00

Specify a second extension line origin or [Undo/Select] <Select>:   **_endp of (3rd mullion line)**

Dimension text = 6000.00

Specify a second extension line origin or [Undo/Select] <Select>:   **Enter**

Select base dimension: **Enter**

You will see that the three dimensions are automatically separated by a spacing of 500, which we set in the **Lines and Arrows/Baseline Spacing** tab.

Continue Dimensions

Because you chose exactly where the door should go, you may get different values, but they should sum to 3900.

■ Use the **Linear Dimension** button to complete the **1900.00** dimension, as shown in Figure 8.9.

■ Use the **Continue Dimension** button to draw in the two **1000.00** dimensions, as shown in Figure 8.9.

Dimension Text Editing

■ Use the **Dimension Text Edit** button to move the **1000.00** figures to a position of your choice. The Command line will prompt

Command: _dimtedit

Select dimension: **(Pick the dimension to move)**

Specify new location for dimension text or [Left/Right/Center/Home/Angle]:   **(Pick new location)**

Angular Dimensions

■ Use the **Angular Dimension** button to measure the wall angle with the text on the dimension arc, as shown in Figure 8.9. Follow the command line prompts to select first and second lines.

Leader Text Dimensions

■ For the wall width description '300mm wall' use the **Quick Leader** button and follow the command line prompts.

*If you need to check a distance between two points in the drawing, but don't want a dimension inserted, use the **Dist** command, which you will find on the **Inquiry** toolbar. The distance between the two points will be displayed on the Command line.*

Practise adding the dimensions shown in Figure 8.11.

Setting the Text Style to Annotate the Drawing

Before adding text to the drawing we must set up a text style. We will set up the same text style as used in the dimensioning style – **Roman Simplex** with a height of **200**.

■ Pick the **FORMAT**/**Text Style** pull-down menu and the **Text Style** dialogue box will appear, as shown in Figure 8.10.

■ Change to the values highlighted.

■ Click on **Apply**.

■ Click on **Close**.

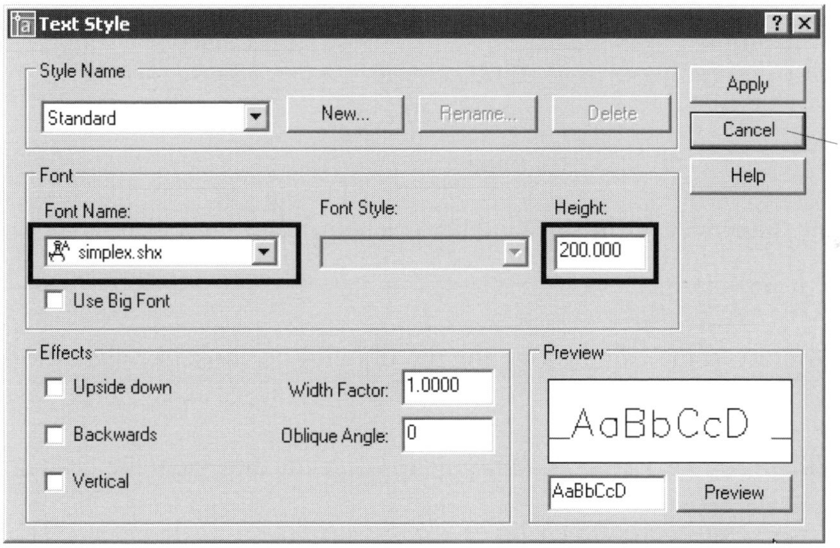

the Cancel button is replaced by Close after Apply is selected

Figure 8.10. *The Text Style dialogue box*

Adding Text to the Drawing

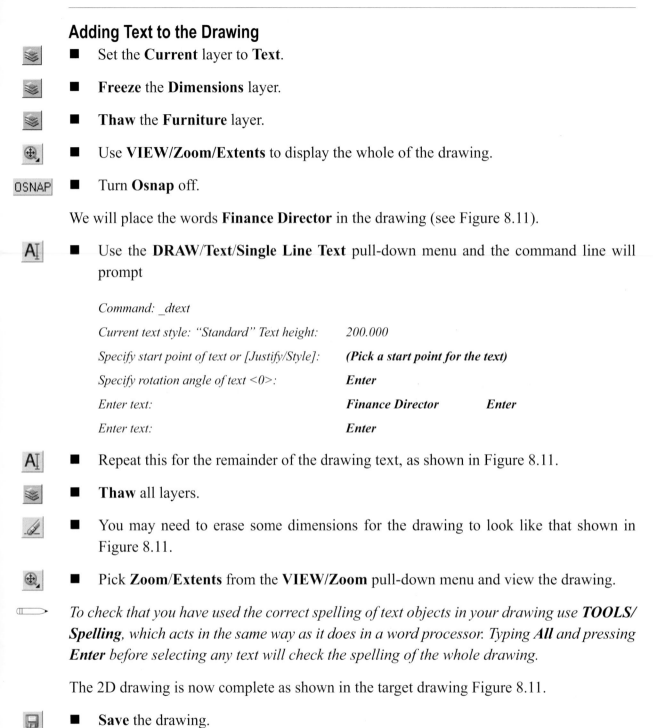

- Set the **Current** layer to **Text**.

- **Freeze** the **Dimensions** layer.

- **Thaw** the **Furniture** layer.

- Use **VIEW/Zoom/Extents** to display the whole of the drawing.

- Turn **Osnap** off.

We will place the words **Finance Director** in the drawing (see Figure 8.11).

- Use the **DRAW/Text/Single Line Text** pull-down menu and the command line will prompt

    Command: _dtext

    Current text style: "Standard" Text height: **200.000**

    Specify start point of text or [Justify/Style]:   **(Pick a start point for the text)**

    Specify rotation angle of text <0>:   **Enter**

    Enter text: **Finance Director**   **Enter**

    Enter text: **Enter**

- Repeat this for the remainder of the drawing text, as shown in Figure 8.11.

- **Thaw** all layers.

- You may need to erase some dimensions for the drawing to look like that shown in Figure 8.11.

- Pick **Zoom/Extents** from the **VIEW/Zoom** pull-down menu and view the drawing.

*To check that you have used the correct spelling of text objects in your drawing use **TOOLS/Spelling**, which acts in the same way as it does in a word processor. Typing **All** and pressing **Enter** before selecting any text will check the spelling of the whole drawing.*

The 2D drawing is now complete as shown in the target drawing Figure 8.11.

- **Save** the drawing.

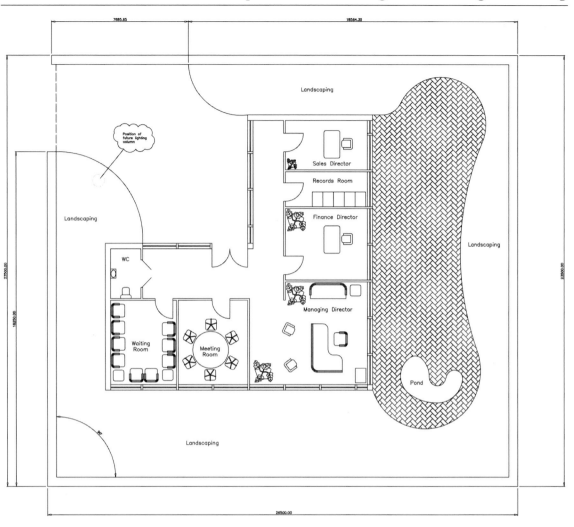

***Figure 8.11.** The 2D plan target drawing showing dimensions and description text*

Creating and Saving Views

A **View** is a 'snapshot' of the display on screen. It can be a magnified area which, if the view is saved, can be returned to without having to use **DISPLAY/Zoom**. Saved **Views** can be printed, which is very useful for presentation purposes.

In this example we will create and save two views: a magnified area of the Managing Director's office, and the Waiting Room.

The saved View changes as the drawing changes; it is not a static snapshot, so if you edit the drawing in any way by adding or deleting objects, the saved View changes.

■ Use **VIEW/Zoom/Object**

Command: '_zoom

Specify corner of window, enter a scale factor (nX or nXP), or

[All/Center/Dynamic/Extents/Previous/Scale/Window/Object] <real time>: _o

Select objects: 1 found	**(Pick a wall, as shown in Figure 8.12)**
Select objects: 1 found, 2 total	**(Pick a wall of the Managing Director's Office)**
Select objects: 1 found, 3 total	**(Pick a wall of the Managing Director's Office)**
Select objects: 1 found, 4 total	**(Pick a wall of the Managing Director's Office)**
Select objects:	**Enter**

The drawing display changes to show the extents of the walls of the office.

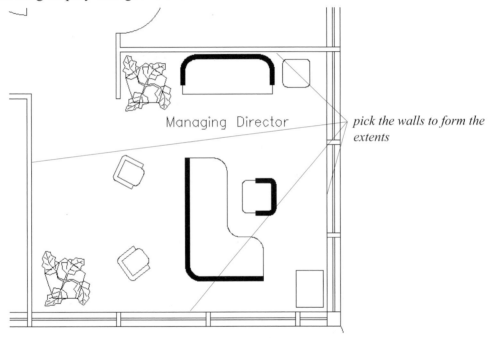

Figure 8.12. *Using the walls of the Managing Director's office to zoom to Objects' extents*

The display will show more than the objects' extents because the objects may not have the same ratio as your screen, as can be seen in Figure 8.13.

We can now save the view of this portion of the drawing.

- ■ Use **VIEW/Named Views** and the **View** dialogue box will appear, as shown in Figure 8.14(a).

- ■ Click on **New**. The **New View** dialogue box will appear, as shown in Figure 8.14(b).

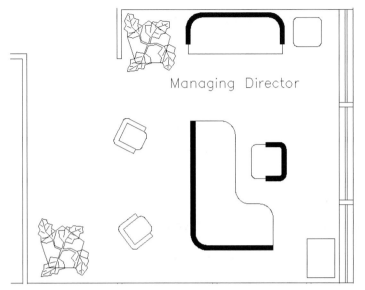

Figure 8.13. *The result of using Zoom to Object when the walls of the Managing Director's office are used as the extents*

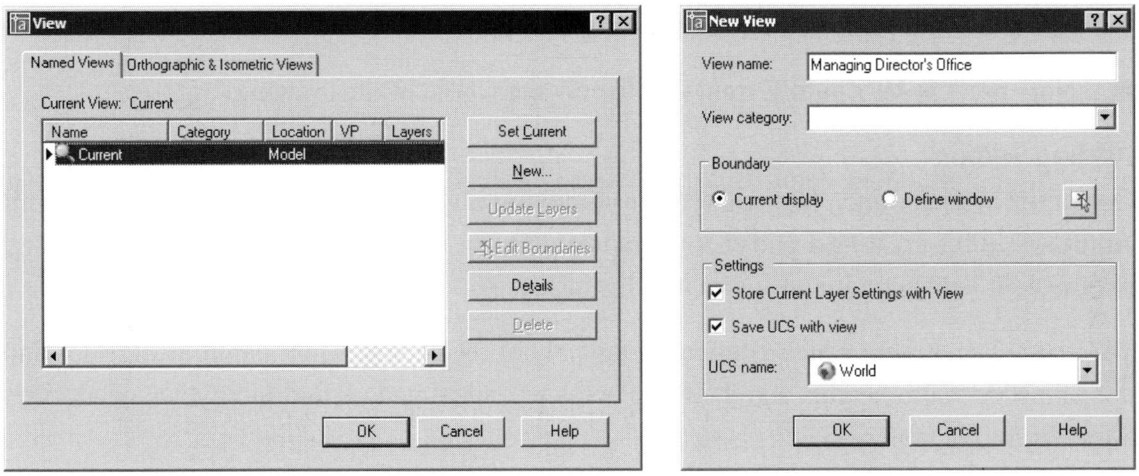

Figure 8.14. *The (a) View and (b) New View dialogue boxes*

■ Type **Managing Director's Office** for the **View name**, as shown in Figure 8.14.

■ Click on **OK**. The **New View** dialogue box will disappear.

■ A new view called **Managing Director's Office** will appear in the window of the **Named Views** tab. Click on **OK** in the **View** dialogue box.

The View is now saved.

- Use **VIEW/Zoom/Extents** to view the extents of the drawing.

- Create a view of the Waiting Room by repeating the above exercise using the walls of the Waiting Room as the extents. Use **VIEW/Named Views** and name the new view as **Waiting Room**.

You should now have the two views listed in the window of the **Named Views** tab.

- Use **VIEW/Zoom/Extents** to show the extents of the drawing.

To check that your saved views are correct, do the following.

- Use **VIEW/Named Views** and in the **View** dialogue box's **Named Views** tab click on **Managing Director's Office**.

- Click on the **Set Current** button and click **OK**.

The display will show the saved view of the **Managing Director's Office**.

- Repeat the exercise to view the **Waiting Room**.

- Now use **VIEW/Zoom/Extents** to display the whole of the drawing.

Adding Tables

One of the most common features seen on a drawing is a specification and parts list. Up until AutoCAD 2005, creating a grid of rows and columns was cumbersome and time-consuming, but the new **Table** command automates this task.

We will create a table which contains details about the rooms: room name, wall, floor and door finishes, room heights and the room areas we calculated earlier. Firstly, we need to set a format for the table.

- Create a new layer called **Roomspec** and make it the **Current** layer.

- **Freeze** all the layers except for **Boundary**, **Roomspec** and **Walls** (although this is not essential).

- Use **VIEW/Zoom/Window** and **Pan** to zoom to an unobstructed part of the drawing. Just outside the boundary wall will be convenient as you can move the completed table to its permanent position after the border sheet is added.

- Pick the **FORMAT/Text Style** pull-down menu and the **Text Style** dialogue box will appear.

- Change the text height to **0**.

- Click on **Apply**, then click on **Close**.

- Use **FORMAT/Table Style** and the **Table Style** dialogue box will appear, as shown in Figure 8.15.

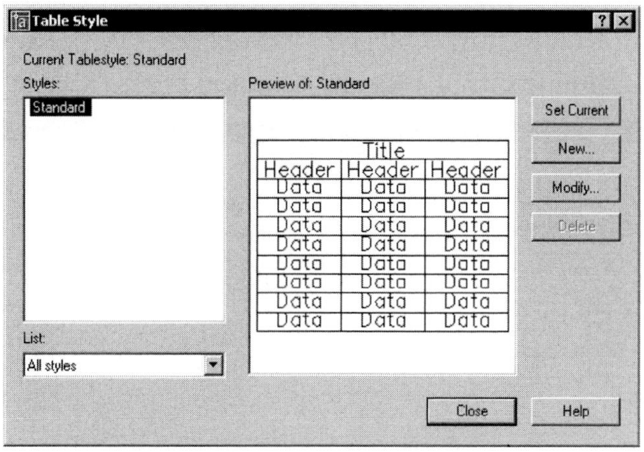

Figure 8.15. The Table Style dialogue box

- Click on the **Modify** button to edit the existing **Standard** style. The **Modify Table Style: Standard** dialogue box appears, as shown in Figure 8.16. It contains three tabs: **Data**, **Column Heads** and **Title**.

- On the **Data** tab change the **Text height** to **100**, as shown in Figure 8.16.

- Repeat the **Text height** change on the **Column Heads** and **Title** tabs ensuring that there is a check in the **Include Title row** box on the **Title** tab.

- Change the **Alignment** to **Middle Center** on all three tabs, as shown in Figure 8.16.

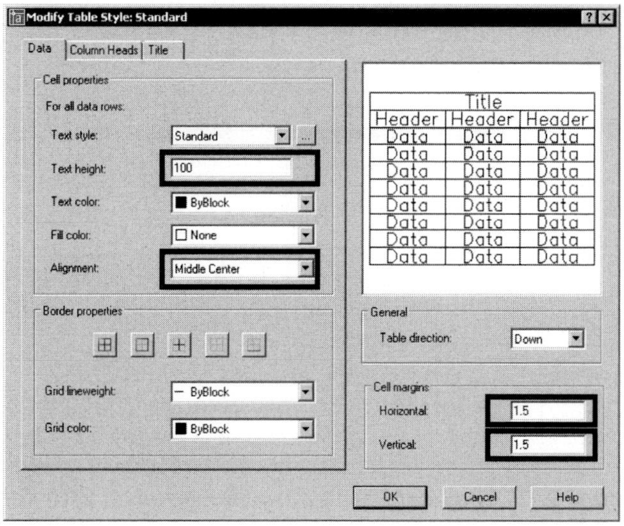

Figure 8.16. The Modify Table Style:Standard dialogue box

107

- Click **OK** and then click **Close** on the **Table Style** dialogue box.

- Use **DRAW/Table** and the **Insert Table** dialogue box will appear, as shown in Figure 8.17.

- Under **Column & Row Settings** enter **6 Columns** and **7 Data Rows** with a **Row height** of **2** lines and **Column width** of **1000**, as shown in Figure 8.17.

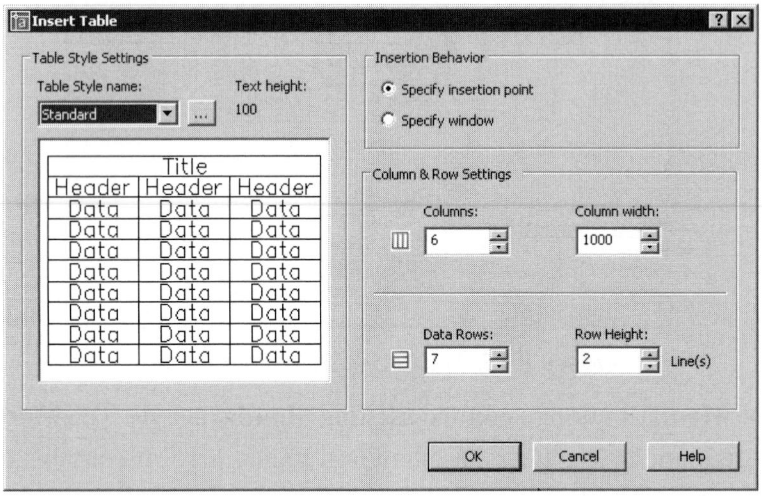

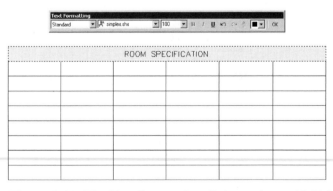

Figure 8.17. The Insert Table dialogue box

- Click **OK**. The **Insert Table** dialogue box disappears and the table outline appears attached to the cursor.

- Pick an insertion point in the drawing.

- The **Text Formatting** dialogue box appears with the table's **Title bar** highlighted and the flashing cursor in the **Middle Center** of the box. Enter the words **ROOM SPECIFICATION,** as shown in Figure 8.18.

Figure 8.18. The Text Formatting dialogue box with Table

- Press **Enter** and the top left cell is highlighted. Enter the word **ROOM**, as shown in Figure 8.19.

- Using the **Tab** key, jump to the next cell and enter **FINISH**.

- Press the **Tab** key three times to create two blank cells and enter **HEIGHT** and lastly **AREA**, as shown in Figure 8.19.

- Click in the cell below **ROOM** and enter the room names, as shown in Figure 8.19.

ROOM SPECIFICATION					
ROOM	FINISH			HEIGHT	AREA
Sales Director					
Record Room					
Finance Director					
Managing Director					
Meeting Room					
Waiting Room					
WC					

Figure 8.19. The table with column and row headings

We need to widen the Room column so that the text in each cell appears on one line.

- Turn **Ortho** on.

ORTHO

- Click once in the **Managing Director** cell (as it is the longest text) and click and drag the right hand grip until the text appears on one line.

- Click **OK** in the **Text Formatting** dialogue bar to close it if it is still on display.

ROOM SPECIFICATION					
ROOM	FINISH			HEIGHT	AREA
Sales Director					
Record Room					
Finance Director					
Managing Director					
Meeting Room					
Waiting Room					
WC					

Figure 8.20. The Managing Director cell highlighted

We now need to merge the Finish cell with the two blank cells to its right and centre the text in the merged cells.

■ Firstly use **TOOLS/Options** to display the **Options** dialogue box. On the **User Preferences** tab ensure that a check is placed in the **Shortcut Menus in drawing area** box, which is found under **Windows Standard Behavior**. This is to ensure that right-clicking the mouse reveals the floating menu when the cells are merged. Click **OK** to exit the **Options** dialogue box.

■ Click once in the **Finish** cell to display the blue grips, then **Shift-click** in the blank cell to the left of the **Height** cell. This action will highlight the **Finish** cell and the two blank cells to its right, as shown in Figure 8.21.

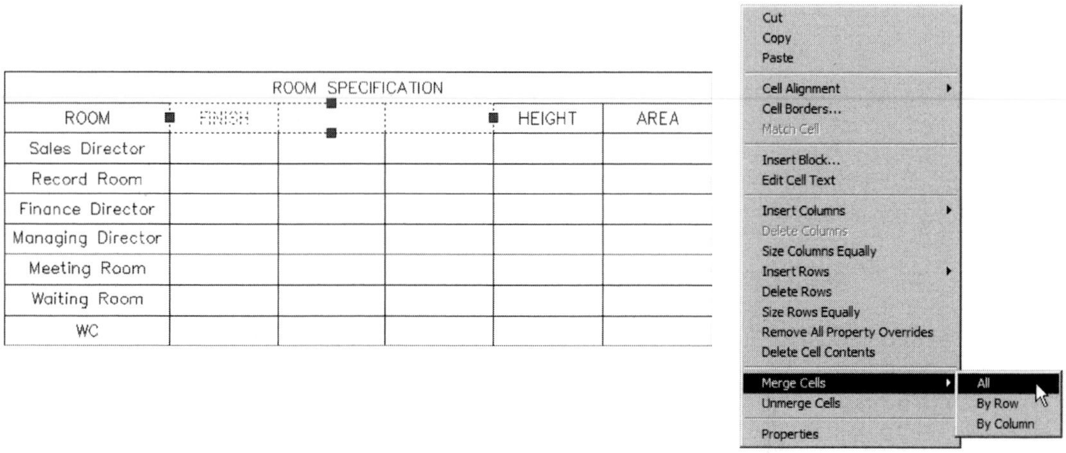

Figure 8.21. The Finish and adjacent cells highlighted and Merge Cells on the floating menu

■ Right-click on the mouse and select **Merge Cells/All** from the floating menu. This will move **Finish** to the centre of the three merged cells.

■ Press **Esc** on the keyboard to hide the grips.

We now need to add a row above the **Sales Director** row.

■ Click in the **Sales Director** cell and right-click. Pick **Insert Rows/Above** from the floating menu and a new row will be inserted.

■ Enter the text **Walls**, **Floor** and **Door** in the cells shown in Figure 8.22.

■ Complete the table, as shown in Figure 8.23 (with your own finishes if preferred).

ROOM SPECIFICATION				
ROOM	FINISH		HEIGHT	AREA
	Walls	Floor	Door		
Sales Director					
Record Room					
Finance Director					
Managing Director					
Meeting Room					
Waiting Room					
WC					

Figure 8.22. The table with Walls, Floor and Door columns added

ROOM SPECIFICATION				
ROOM	FINISH		HEIGHT	AREA
	Walls	Floor	Door		
Sales Director	White Matt	Carpet	Light Oak	2800	12.42
Record Room	White Matt	Tile	Light Oak	2800	8.74
Finance Director	White Matt	Carpet	Light Oak	2800	17.94
Managing Director	White Matt	Carpet	Light Oak	2800	34.96
Meeting Room	White Matt	Carpet	Light Oak	2800	17.94
Waiting Room	White Matt	Carpet	Light Oak	2800	17.02
WC	White Matt	Tile	Light Oak	2800	4.59

Figure 8.23. The Table with completed data entered

Lastly, we will change the cell border line thicknesses to emphasise the title bar and column headings.

- Use **FORMAT/Lineweight** and the **Lineweight Settings** dialogue box will appear.

- Ensure that you put a check in the **Display Lineweight** box, as shown in Figure 8.24.

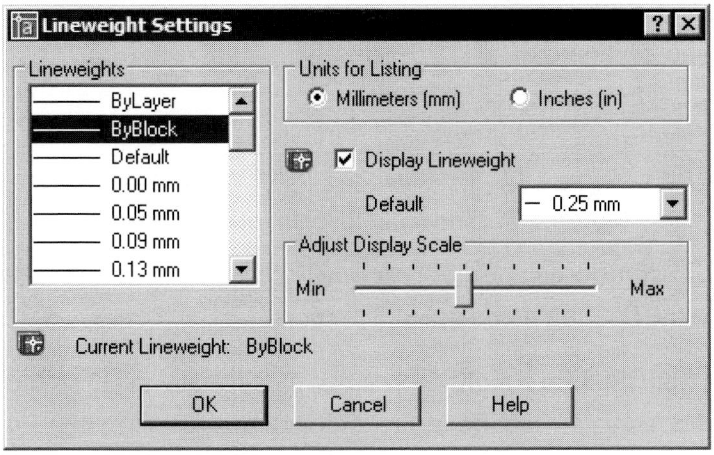

Figure 8.24. The Lineweight Settings dialogue box

- Click **OK** and the **Lineweight Settings** dialogue box will disappear.

- Click inside the title cell (inside the cell, not on the line) and the grips will appear.

111

- Shift-click in the bottom right cell and the grips will appear at the edges of the whole table.

- Right-click and pick **Cell Borders** from the floating menu.

- The **Cell Border Properties** dialogue box appears, as shown in Figure 8.25.

- Pick **0.35mm** from the **Lineweight** drop-down menu and click the **Outside Borders** button from the **Apply to** section of the dialogue box, as shown in Figure 8.25.

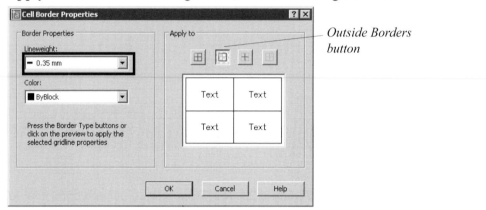

Figure 8.25. The Cell Border Properties dialogue box

- Click **OK** and the table border now has a width of 0.35mm, as shown in Figure 8.26.

ROOM SPECIFICATION					
ROOM	FINISH			HEIGHT	AREA
	Walls	Floor	Door		
Sales Director	White Matt	Carpet	Light Oak	2800	12.42
Record Room	White Matt	Tile	Light Oak	2800	8.74
Finance Director	White Matt	Carpet	Light Oak	2800	17.94
Managing Director	White Matt	Carpet	Light Oak	2800	34.96
Meeting Room	White Matt	Carpet	Light Oak	2800	17.94
Waiting Room	White Matt	Carpet	Light Oak	2800	17.02
WC	White Matt	Tile	Light Oak	2800	4.59

Figure 8.26. The table 0.35mm outside border

- To apply a **0.35mm** border to the **Title bar**, click inside it, right-click and pick **Cell Borders** from the floating menu again.

- Pick **0.35mm** from the **Lineweight** drop-down menu again and click the **Outside Borders** button from the **Apply to** section of the dialogue box, as shown in Figure 8.25.

- Apply a **0.35mm** border to the **Column Headings** by clicking inside the **Room** cell and **Shift-clicking** in the **Area** cell to select the entire row.

■ Pick **0.35mm** from the **Lineweight** drop-down menu again and click the **Outside Borders** button from the **Apply to** section of the dialogue box and the table is complete, as shown in Figure 8.27.

■ Press **Esc** on the keyboard to remove the grips.

ROOM SPECIFICATION					
ROOM	FINISH			HEIGHT	AREA
	Walls	Floor	Door		
Sales Director	White Matt	Carpet	Light Oak	2800	12.42
Record Room	White Matt	Tile	Light Oak	2800	8.74
Finance Director	White Matt	Carpet	Light Oak	2800	17.94
Managing Director	White Matt	Carpet	Light Oak	2800	34.96
Meeting Room	White Matt	Carpet	Light Oak	2800	17.94
Waiting Room	White Matt	Carpet	Light Oak	2800	17.02
WC	White Matt	Tile	Light Oak	2800	4.59

Figure 8.27. The completed Table

To change the contents of a cell, select the cell, right-click and pick ***Edit Cell Text.***

Use ***TOOLS/Options*** *to display the* ***Options*** *dialogue box. On the* ***User Preferences*** *tab ensure that the check is removed in the* ***Shortcut Menus in drawing area*** *box, which is found under* ***Windows Standard Behavior.***

ORTHO ■ Turn **Ortho** off.

■ **Save** the drawing.

Chapter 9 – Changing the View of the Drawing from 2D to 3D

S o far we have worked and drawn in 2D, looking from directly above the drawing in a planimetric view. To make it easier to change objects from 2D to 3D we shall view the drawing initially from a **South-East Isometric** viewpoint.

We shall change the height of the end walls, internal partitions and mullions to 2800mm, and of the walls between the mullions to 700mm to form low sills.

- Make the **Roof** layer **Current**.

- **Freeze** all layers except for **Roof**, **Walls** and **Windows**.

- From the **VIEW/Toolbars** pull-down menu load the **View** toolbar.

- Pick the **SE Isometric View** button and the drawing will appear, as shown in Figure 9.1.

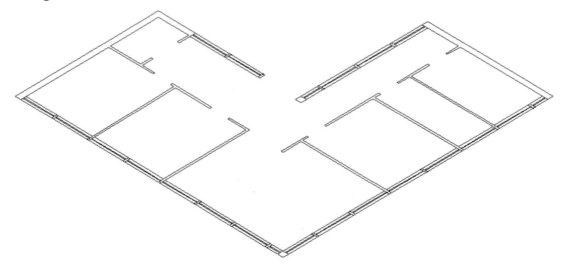

Figure 9.1. A South-East Isometric view

Creating 3D from 2D

We will use the **Chprop/Thickness** command to give height to selected objects in the drawing.

- You will probably need to use **VIEW/Zoom/Window** to enlarge portions of the drawing to complete the change of thicknesses, as shown in Figure 9.3.

- Type **chprop** at the command line

> *Command:* ***chprop*** ***Enter***
>
> *Select objects: 78 found* **(Pick the end walls, internal partitions and mullions)**
>
> *Select objects:* ***Enter***
>
> *Enter property to change [Color/LAyer/LType/ltScale/LWeight/Thickness]: t (for thickness)*
>
> *Specify new thickness <0.000>:* ***2800*** ***Enter***
>
> *Enter property to change [Color/LAyer/LType/ltScale/LWeight/Thickness]:* ***Enter***

*Whilst picking the end walls, internal positions and mullions you may inadvertently pick an object. Enter **R** (for **Remove**) where the **Command Line** says **Select Objects** and pick the object. This will remove the object from the selection set and the object will become a solid line instead of broken. Enter **A** (for **Add**) at the **Command Line** to add further objects.*

*Another method of changing properties, but with the same result, is to use the **MODIFY/ Properties** toolbar.*

- Pick one or more of the walls between the mullions. **Grips** (small blue squares) will appear on the objects.

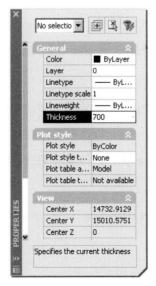

***Figure 9.2.** The Properties Palette dialogue box*

- Pick **MODIFY/Properties** and the **Properties** dialogue box will appear, as shown in Figure 9.2.

- Change the **Thickness** value to 700.

- Close the dialogue box.

- The thickness of the objects will be changed. Press **Esc** to clear the **Grips**.

Using either method, repeat the operation to give the rest of the walls between the mullions a **Thickness** of **700mm**, as shown in Figure 9.3.

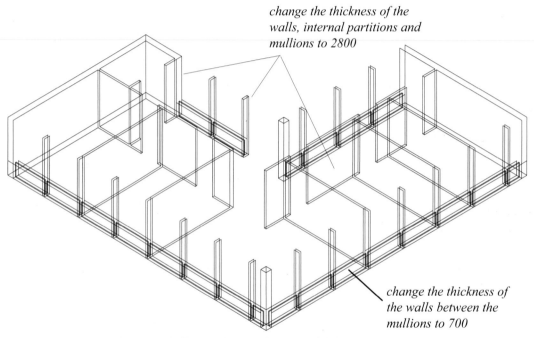

change the thickness of the walls, internal partitions and mullions to 2800

change the thickness of the walls between the mullions to 700

Figure 9.3. The building after the Thickness command

Making the Drawing Look Solid

When you have completed changing the **Thickness**, your drawing will appear as a 'wireframe', as shown in Figure 9.3.

- To make the drawing appear solid, use the **VIEW/Hide** command. The drawing will appear as in Figure 9.4.

*When you change your view, by **Pan** or **Zoom** for example, you will need to use **VIEW/Hide** again to produce a solid view.*

We are now ready to draw the outline of the roof.

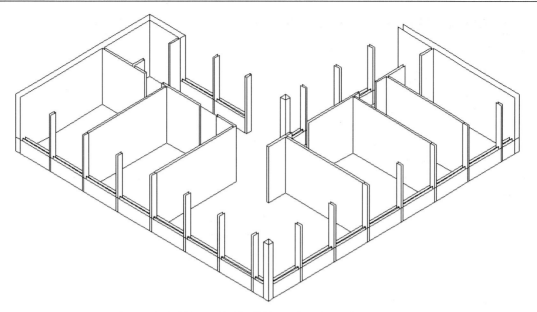

Figure 9.4. The solid building after the Hide command

To Draw the Roof

■ Ensure that the **Roof** layer is **Current**.

■ Use **DRAW/Line** to draw a line around the perimeter of the building picking the **Endpoints** or **Intersections** of the corners, as shown in Figure 9.5.

draw to the Endpoints or Intersections around the perimeter

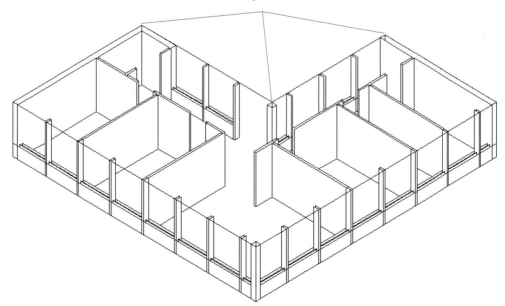

Figure 9.5. The perimeter of the roof

Drawing with 3D Coordinates

So far we have used two-dimensional coordinates X and Y, to draw the objects in the drawing. Three-dimensional coordinates include Z so that the coordinates become X,Y, Z where Z is the height from base level. We have just changed the Z value of the walls and mullions.

We will use X, Y, Z **absolute coordinates** to draw the ridge line of the roof.

- Use **DRAW/Line** to draw the roof ridge line and the command line will prompt

Command: _line Specify first point:	***5000,10000,5600***	***Enter***
Specify next point or [Undo]:	***16500,10000,5600***	***Enter***
Specify next point or [Undo]:	***16500,21000,5600***	***Enter***
Specify next point or [Close/Undo]:	***Enter***	

The drawing will now look like Figure 9.6.

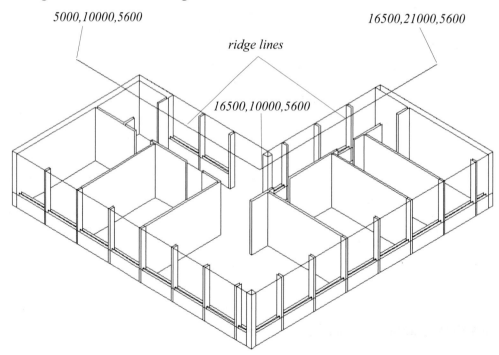

5000,10000,5600   *16500,21000,5600*

ridge lines

16500,10000,5600

Figure 9.6. The drawn ridge line

- **Freeze** all layers except for the **Roof** layer.

- To complete the roof, draw the gable ends and the hips, as shown in Figure 9.7, using the **Endpoints** or **Intersections** of the previously drawn roof lines.

Draw the gable ends and the hips

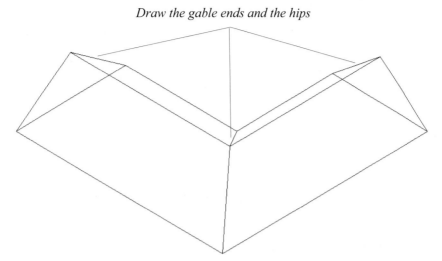

Figure 9.7. The completed roof with gable ends and hips

Making the Roof Solid

We have created the roof by simply joining lines together in 3D space. The roof will not present a solid appearance like the walls until a surface is applied. (The wall surfaces were applied automatically with the **Thickness** command.)

We will use the **3DFace** command to apply an invisible surface or skin to the different roof planes so that when we use the **Hide** command the roof will appear solid. The second reason for doing this is so that when we apply a **Hatch** to appear as roof tiles, the hatching will not appear 'see-through'. (AutoCAD LT users should use the **Solid** command with **Fill** turned **Off**.)

Prior to hatching, the drawing plane will be changed from a **World Coordinate System (WCS)** to a **User Coordinate System (UCS)**, whose position in 3D space can be saved.

- Create a layer called **3DFace** with a colour of your choice.

- Make **3DFace** the **Current** layer.

- Use **VIEW/Toolbars** to load the **Surfaces** toolbar.

- Move the **Surfaces** toolbar to a convenient position on screen.

■ Click on the **3D Face** button and the command line will prompt

Command: _3dface

Specify first point or [Invisible]:	**_int of (Pick, as shown in Figure 9.8)**
Specify second point or [Invisible]:	**_int of (Pick, as shown in Figure 9.8)**
Specify third point or [Invisible] <exit>:	**_int of (Pick, as shown in Figure 9.8)**
Specify fourth point or [Invisible] <create three-sided face>:	**_int of (Pick, as shown in Figure 9.8)**
Specify third point or [Invisible] <exit>:	**Enter**

■ Repeat this for all the surfaces of the roof including the gable ends, which are triangular so have only three **Intersection** pick points.

■ Close the **Surfaces** toolbar when complete.

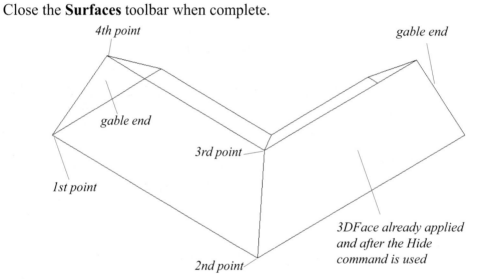

Figure 9.8. The results of the 3DFace command

Changing to a User Coordinate System

Before applying the roof tile hatching we must change the drawing planes to coincide with the roof pitches using the **UCS/3Point** command, which repositions the X,Y and Z directions.

■ Use **VIEW/Toolbars** to load the **UCS** toolbar.

■ Pick the **3 point UCS** option and the command line will prompt

> *Command: _ucs*
>
> *Current ucs name: *WORLD**
>
> *Enter an option [New/Move/orthoGraphic/Prev/Restore/Save/Del/Apply/?/World] <World>:_3*
>
> *Specify new origin point <0,0,0>:*   **_int of (Pick as shown in Figure 9.9)**
>
> *Specify point on positive portion of X-axis <5001.000,6000.000,2800.000>:*
>
> **_int of (Pick as shown in Figure 9.9)**
>
> *Specify point on positive-Y portion of the UCS XY plane <5000.000,6001.000,2800.000>:*
>
> **_int of (Pick as shown in Figure 9.9)**

Your drawing should now look like Figure 9.9.

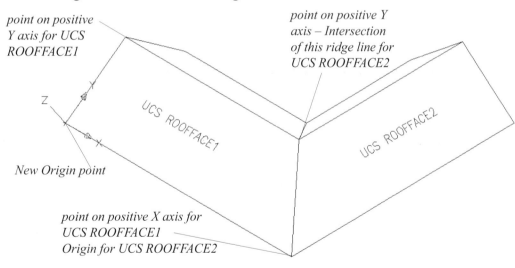

point on positive Y axis for UCS ROOFFACE1

point on positive Y axis – Intersection of this ridge line for UCS ROOFFACE2

New Origin point

point on positive X axis for UCS ROOFFACE1
Origin for UCS ROOFFACE2

Figure 9.9. *The new UCS position*

*If the **UCS** icon is not positioned over the new origin, type **UCSicon** at the command line and enter the **Or** for **Origin** option, which will place the icon at the new origin as shown in Figure 9.9. Use **VIEW/Zoom Out** also.*

*The style of the **UCS** icon (see page 3, Figures 1.3 and 1.4) can be changed from 2D to 3D and vice versa. To do this, use **VIEW/Display/UCS icon/Properties** and in the **UCS icon style** rectangle click on the 2D or 3D radio buttons. The change of style will be shown in the **Preview** pane.*

Saving the UCS Position

- It is a good idea to save this new drawing plane position: pick the **UCS** button and the command line will prompt

  Command: ucs

  Current ucs name: *NO NAME*

  *Enter an option [New/Move/orthoGraphic/Prev/Restore/Save/Del/Apply/?/World] <World>: **s (for save)***

  Enter name to save current UCS or [?]:   ***UCSROOFFACE1***

- For **UCSROOFFACE2** repeat the process of defining the roof plane as before but with the positive portion on the **Y** axis being the **Intersection** of the ridge lines as shown in the construction of **UCSROOFFACE2** in Figure 9.9.

- Use **UCS/Save** to save the position with the name **UCSROOFFACE2**.

- Change the view of the drawing by picking the **NW Isometric View** button.

- Repeat the process of creating the UCS drawing planes for **UCSROOFFACE3** and **UCSROOFFACE4,** as shown in Figure 9.10.

*When you define **UCSROOFFACE4** the positive portion on the **Y** axis is **Perpendicular** to the ridge, as shown in Figure 9.10.*

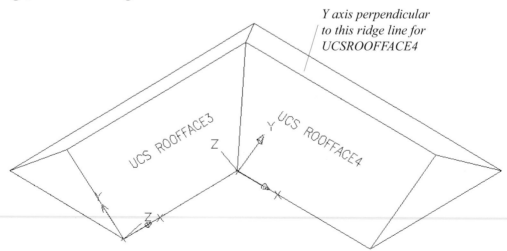

Figure 9.10. *The NW Isometric View position with the new drawing planes*

■ Save the **UCS** positions with the names **UCSROOFFACE3** and **UCSROOFFACE4,** as shown in Figure 9.10.

Changing the UCS

Once you have created the **UCSs** you will need to alternate between them. In readiness for hatching the roof we will reinstate **UCSROOFFACE1**.

Firstly, we will change the view of the drawing.

■ Pick the **SE Isometric View** button.

■ Pick the **Display UCS Dialog** button and the **UCS** dialogue box will appear, as shown in Figure 9.11.

■ Click on **UCSROOFFACE1** and **Set Current**.

■ Click on **OK**.

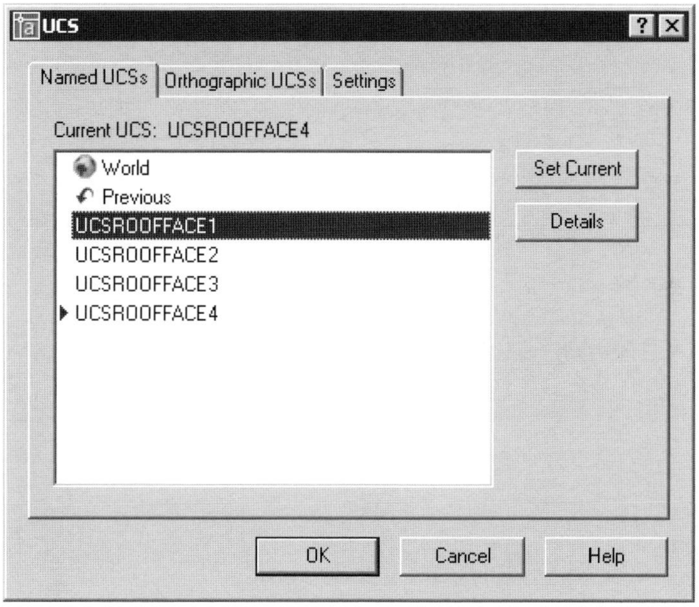

Figure 9.11. The UCS dialogue box

UCSROOFFACE1 is now the current **UCS** and the **UCS** icon should be placed at its origin position, as shown in Figure 9.9.

Hatching the Roof

- **Thaw** the **Roofhatch** layer and make it **Current**.

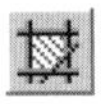

- Use **DRAW**/**Hatch** and the **Boundary Hatch and Fill** dialogue box will appear as shown in Figure 9.12.

- Click on the **Pattern** drop-down menu and select the **AR-B88** style.

- Click on **Pick Points**. The dialogue box disappears and the command line will prompt

  Command: _bhatch

  Select internal point: Selecting everything...   **(Click within UCSROOFFACE1)**

  Selecting everything visible...

  Analyzing the selected data...

  Analyzing internal islands...

  Select internal point: **Enter**

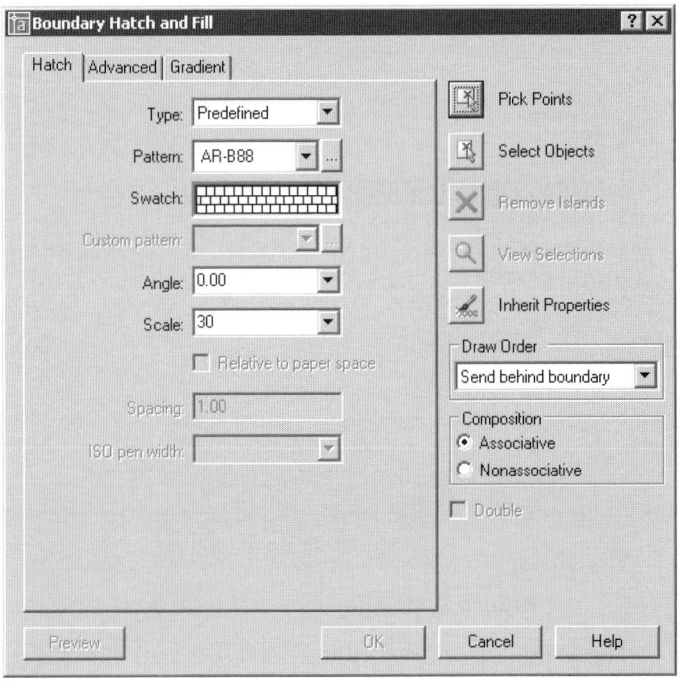

Figure 9.12. The Boundary Hatch and Fill pallette with AR-B88 selected

- The **Boundary Hatch and Fill** dialogue box reappears. You can now either look at the hatch pattern in situ with **Preview** or you can **OK** the pattern. **Preview** gives the opportunity to change the pattern and scale before finally clicking on **OK**.

- Change the **Scale** to anything between 1 and 30 for a more or less dense pattern.

*If clicking on **Pick Points** gives a **'Valid hatch boundary not found'** message, use the **Select objects** button to pick the edge of the roof outline.*

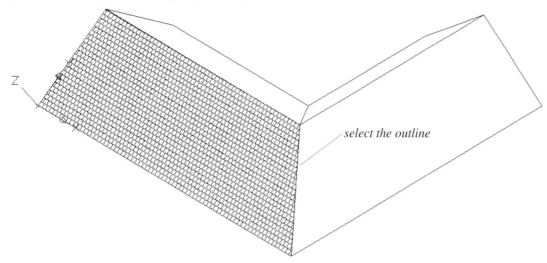

select the outline

Figure 9.13. ROOFFACE1 hatched

- Restore **UCSROOFFACE2** and **Set Current** and **Hatch** that plane, as shown in Figure 9.14.

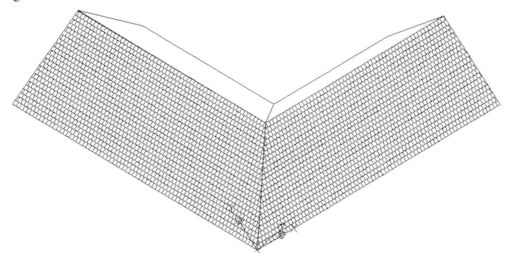

Figure 9.14. ROOFFACE2 hatched

- Pick the **NW Isometric View** button.

- Restore **UCSROOFFACE3** and **Hatch** that plane.

- Restore **UCSROOFFACE4** and **Hatch** that plane.

The drawing should now look like Figure 9.15.

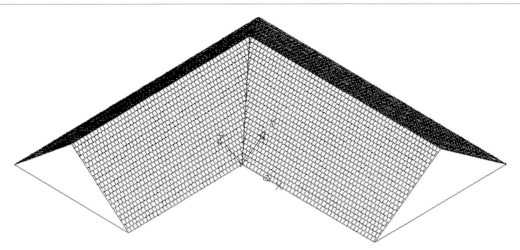

Figure 9.15. The completed roof hatching

- Select the **Display UCS Dialog** button, and in the **UCS** dialogue box click on **World** and **Set Current**.

- Click on **OK**.

- Close the **UCS** toolbar.

- **Thaw** all the layers except **Dimensions**, **Doors**, **Drivewayedge**, **Exterior Lighting**, **Furniture**, **Roomspec**, and **Text**.

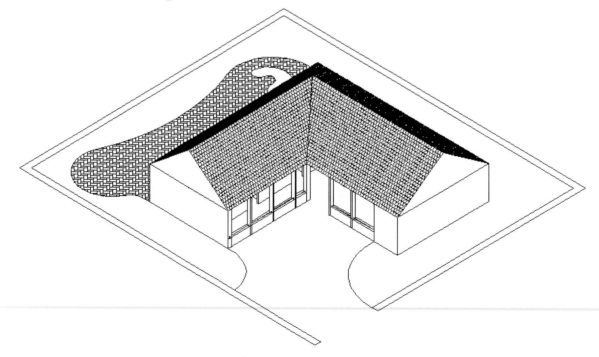

Figure 9.16. The completed building looking from the NW isometric

■ Make layer **0 Current**.

■ Use **VIEW/Zoom/Extents** and **VIEW/Hide** to display the drawing as shown in Figure 9.16.

To View the Completed 2D Target Drawing

■ From the **VIEW** pull-down menu select **3DViews/Plan View/World UCS**.

■ **Freeze** the **Roof**, **Roofhatch** and **3DFace** layers.

■ **Thaw** the **Doors** and **Furniture** layers and the plan view of the drawing should look like Figure 9.17.

■ **Save** the drawing.

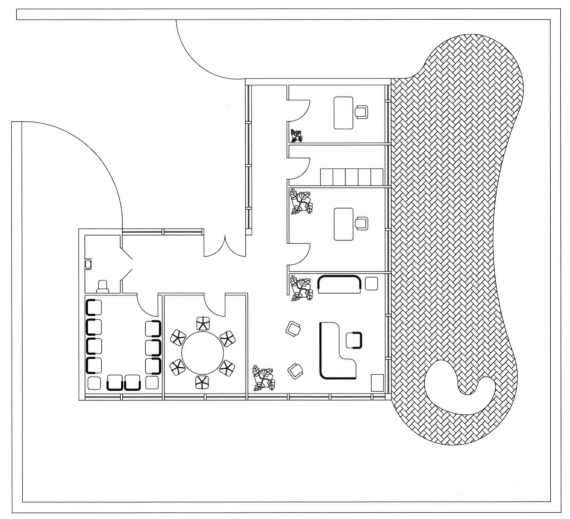

Figure 9.17. The completed plan of the building

Chapter 10 – Paper Space and Plotting

We have completed our drawing in what is known as **Model Space**. If several tiled viewports are displayed, editing in one viewport affects all other viewports. (We have only used one viewport throughout the drawing.) However, you can set magnification, viewpoint, grid, and snap settings individually for each viewport.

The first time you switch to **Paper Space**, the graphics area displays a blank space that represents the 'paper' on which you arrange your drawing. In this space, you create **floating viewports** to contain different views of your model, as shown in Figure 10.1.

In **Paper Space**, floating viewports are treated as objects that you can move and resize in order to create a suitable layout. You are not restricted to plotting a single **Model Space** view, as you are with **tiled viewports**. Therefore, any arrangement of floating viewports can be plotted. In **Paper Space**, you can also draw objects, such as title blocks or annotations, directly in the **Paper Space** view without affecting the model itself.

Model Space and **Paper Space** differ in that **Paper Space** accepts values at a 1:1 ratio so that if you wanted the title of the drawing to be in 10mm-high text, in **Paper Space** you would select 10mm-high text. In **Model Space** the text height would have to be a multiple of the final

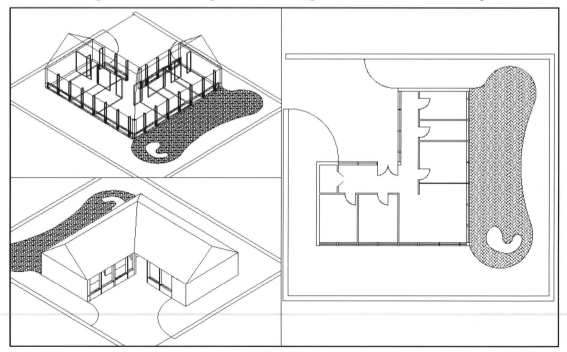

Figure 10.1. Three different views of the building on one drawing shown with floating viewports

plotted scale of the drawing; for example, 10mm-high text at scale of 1:50 would be entered at a size of 10×50 = 500mm. When you plot from **Paper Space** the scale is 1:1.

AutoCAD allows us to set up a pre-drawn border in **Paper Space**, using the **Wizards/ Advanced Setup** facility, when a new drawing is started. We have not approached drawing in this way, so we will insert the pre-drawn border in **Paper Space** using **Xref**, complete the border drawing information (such as the titling) and create three floating viewports with views as shown in Figure 10.2.

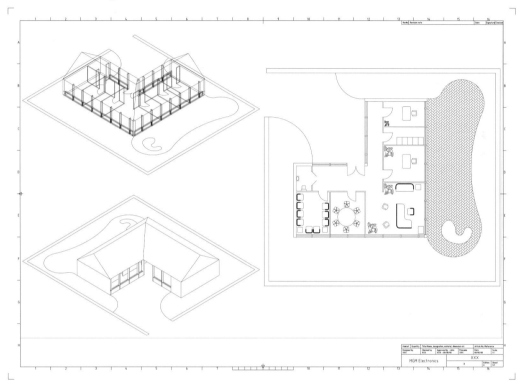

Figure 10.2. The completed drawing in Paper Space with inserted pre-drawn border and details, with viewport boundaries frozen

Changing to Paper Space

■ Firstly, use **TOOLS/Options** and the **Options** dialogue box will appear. Click the **Display** tab and under **Layout Elements** uncheck **Create viewport in new layouts**. Click **OK**.

■ To change to **Paper Space** click the **Model** button on the **Status bar,** as shown in Figure 10.3, or click on the **Layout1** tab.

The drawing will disappear leaving a blank screen. The **Paper Space** icon appears in the bottom left corner and **Paper** shows on the **Status bar** in place of **Model**. The **Layout1** tab will also be active.

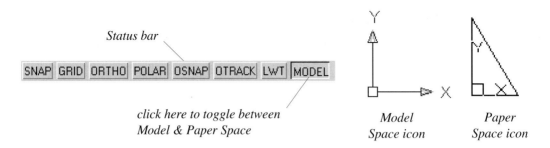

Status bar

SNAP GRID ORTHO POLAR OSNAP OTRACK LWT MODEL

*click here to toggle between
Model & Paper Space*

*Model
Space icon*

*Paper
Space icon*

Figure 10.3. *The Model Space & Tile toggle buttons with the Paper Space and Model Space icons*

*If a printer/plotter is not configured, the first time you change to **Paper Space** the **Page Setup** dialogue box appears. Set up the plotter type, paper size, and so on. Click on **OK**.*

*To return to **Model Space** click on the **Paper** button at any time. If you have not created viewports in **Paper Space** this will not work – you must click on the **Model** tab.*

*The **Paper Space** layout may display a dotted line around the perimeter of the paper background. To disable this feature use **TOOLS/Options** and click on the **Display** tab. Under the **Layout Elements** section uncheck **Display printable area** and **Display paper background**. Click on **OK**.*

External References

When we made the blocks for the furniture we used the **Insert** command to place the symbols in the drawing. Another method of doing this is to insert a drawing as an external reference. There are important differences between blocks and external references.

An **External Reference** (**Xref**) is not part of the drawing, but is loaded at the same time as the drawing. Whilst it appears on screen it does not increase the drawing size, so storage on the hard drive is not increased. Another useful feature is that when an external reference – a drawing in its own right – is changed in any way, that change is shown in all of the drawings in which the external reference appears.

If a drawing has an external reference, the **Status bar** will show the **Manage Xrefs** icon directly next to the **Communication Center** icon, as shown in Figure 10.4.

the Manage Xrefs icon

Figure 10.4. *The Reference icon on the right of the Status bar*

Inserting the Pre-Drawn Border Using an External Reference

*Before inserting the pre-drawn template border we need to locate the Template folder, which is stored in a new position in AutoCAD 2005. Use **TOOLS/Options** to display the **Options** dialogue box. Click on the **Files** tab. Double-click on **Template Settings** and double-click again on **Drawing Template File Location**. This will reveal the path of the **Template** folder. Make a note of this path as it is fairly long and we shall need it shortly. Click **OK** to close the Options dialogue box. (Alternatively the drawing is available from the publisher's website at www.payne-gallway.co.uk.)*

- Ensure that you are in **Paper Space**.

- Create a layer called **Border**.

- Make **Border** the **Current** layer.

- From the **Insert** pull-down menu pick **External Reference**. The **Select Reference File** dialogue box will appear, as shown in Figure 10.5.

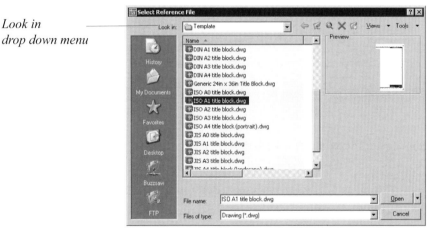

Look in drop down menu

Figure 10.5. The Select Reference File dialogue box

- Use the **Look in** drop-down menu to locate the path of the **Template** folder you have already made a note of (or the location of the drawing after you have downloaded it from the publisher's website).

*If you cannot see the **Local Settings** folder, open Windows Explorer and use **TOOLS/Folder Options**. In the **View** tab change the settings for **Hidden files and folders** to **Show hidden files and folders** and click on **OK**.*

- Select the drawing called **ISO A1 title block.dwg** and click on **Open**. The **Select Reference File** dialogue box will disappear and the **External Reference** dialogue box will appear, as shown in Figure 10.6.

- Uncheck **Specify on Screen** so that the insertion point of the drawing becomes preset at **(0,0,0)** coordinates, as shown in Figure 10.6.

- Click on **OK**.

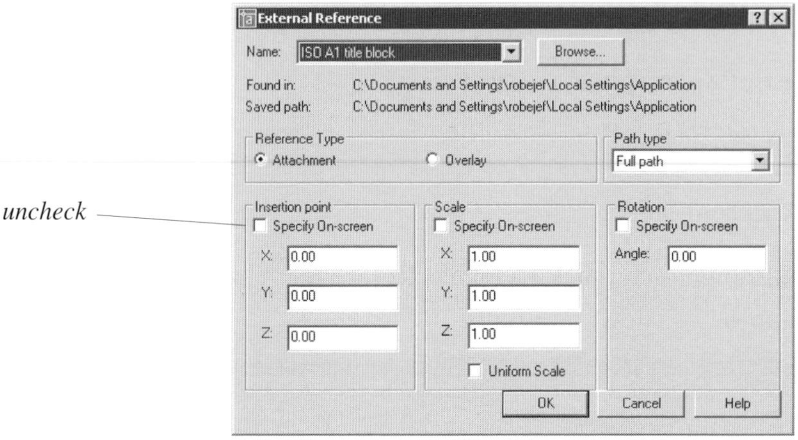

Figure 10.6. The External Reference dialogue box

- Use **VIEW/Zoom/Window** and **Pan** to enlarge the title box area, as shown in Figure 10.7.

- Create a new layer called **PStext** and make it **Current**.

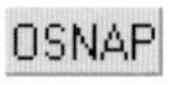

- Ensure that **Osnap** is off.

- Use **FORMAT/Text Style** and in the **Text Style** dialogue box set the height to **5**.

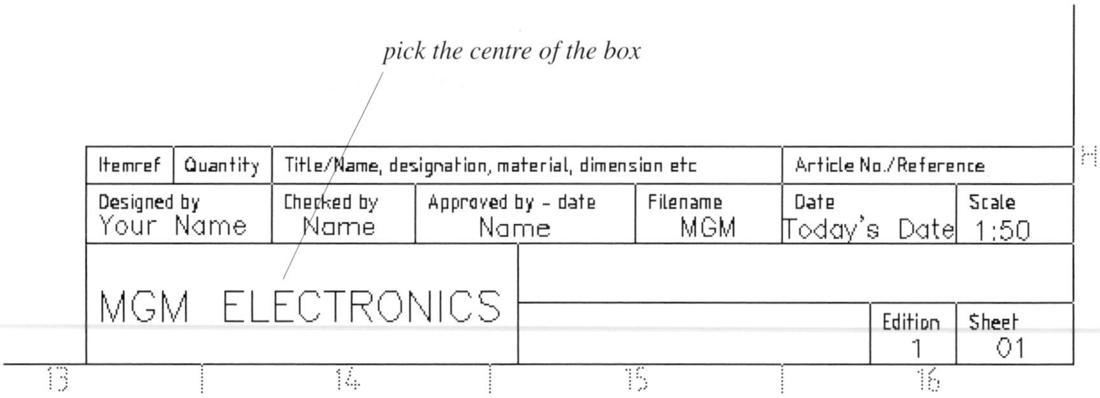

Figure 10.7. The title box of the Inserted ISO A1 title block drawing

■ Click **Apply** and then **Close**.

■ From the pull-down menu **DRAW/Text** select **Single Line Text**. The command line will prompt

Command: *_dtext*

Current text style: "Standard" Text height: *5.000*

Specify start point of text or [Justify/Style]:   ***j (for Justify)   Enter***

*Enter an option [Align/Fit/Center/Middle/Right/TL/TC/TR/ML/MC/MR/BL/BC/BR]: **c (for Centre) Enter***

Specify center point of text: **(Pick the centre of the box, as shown in Figure 10.7)**

Specify rotation angle of text <0>:   ***Enter***

Enter text: ***MGM ELECTRONICS   Enter***

Enter text: ***Enter***

The words MGM ELECTRONICS will appear, as shown in Figure 10.7.

■ Add details into the other boxes. You will need to reduce the text size to suit.

■ **Zoom Extents** so that all of the border drawing is visible.

Creating Viewports

■ Create a new layer called **PSvports** and make it **Current** with a prominent colour.

■ From the pull-down menu **VIEW/Viewports** select **3 Viewports** and the command line will prompt

Command: _-vports

Specify corner of viewport [ON/OFF/Fit/Shadeplot/Lock/Object/Polygonal/Restore/2/3/4]<Fit>: _3

*Enter viewport arrangement [Horizontal/Vertical/Above/Below/Left/Right] <Right>: **Enter***

Specify first corner or [Fit] <Fit>:   **(Pick corner, as shown in Figure 10.8)**

Specify opposite corner: **(Pick corner, as shown in Figure 10.8)**

Regenerating model.

The drawing will appear as shown in Figure 10.8 with the same view of the drawing in all three viewports.

pick first corner near border corner

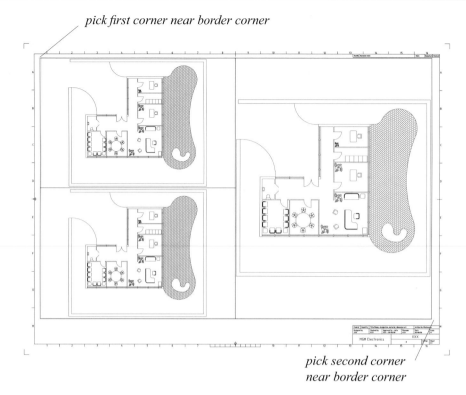

pick second corner near border corner

Figure 10.8. *Three floating viewports in Paper Space*

Moving Between Model Space and Paper Space

AutoCAD does not allow us to edit the drawing in **Paper Space** so we need to return to **Model Space** to change the views in the left hand viewports.

PAPER

- Click on **Paper** in the **Status bar** to activate **Model Space** tiled viewports.

- Click on the top left viewport to make it the current active viewport, which is indicated with a thicker outline than the other viewports.

- Use one of the **Isometric View** buttons to choose a suitable view of your drawing, as shown in Figure 10.9. You may need to **Zoom** or **Pan** to obtain a view to your liking.

- Use your own judgement to decide what layers you would like to display in the viewports.

- To **Freeze** layers in the current viewport, open the **Layer Properties Manager** dialogue box and click on the layer name followed by clicking on the **Current VP Freeze** 'sun' in the same line.

You may need to widen the dialogue box by clicking and dragging the column separator to reveal this part of the Layer Properties Manager.

134

- Click on **OK**. Any selected layers will now only be frozen in the currently active viewport.

- Repeat the operation for the bottom left viewport to produce a view and visible layers, as shown in Figure 10.9.

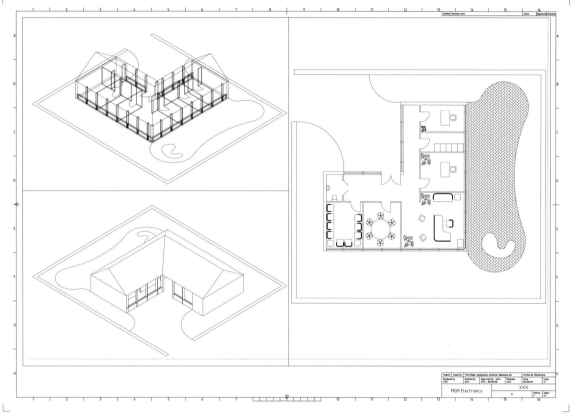

Figure 10.9. The completed drawing showing views with viewport boundaries frozen

- Click on the **Model** button to return to **Paper Space**.

To view the drawing without viewports visible we need to make another layer **Current** in order to **Freeze** the **PSvports** layer.

- Make layer **0 Current**.

- **Freeze** the **PSvports** layer.

- **Save** the drawing

The completed drawing will appear similar to that shown in Figure 10.9 and is now ready for plotting.

Plotting the Drawing

Assuming a plotter or printer is attached and has been configured, do the following.

■ Use **FILE/Plot**. The **Plot** dialogue box appears, as shown in Figure 10.10. (Click on the **More Options** button, next to the **Help** button, to fully expand the dialogue box.)

■ From the **What to plot** drop-down menu select **Extents**.

■ Set a **Plot Scale** of **1:1**.

■ Select a **Paper size** of **ISO A1 (841.00 x 594 MM)**. (If you are using a smaller plotter or a printer then place a check in **Fit to paper**. Use this option only for presentation – it is never advisable to take scaled measurements from such a plot.)

■ In **Plot Offset** place a check in the **Center the plot** box.

■ Place a check in the **Hide Paperspace Objects** box, which hides the hidden lines on 3D drawings, as shown in Figure 10.10.

■ Activate a **Preview** to check the plot is correct.

■ When you are satisfied, load the plotter or printer with the plotting media.

■ Click on **OK** to plot the drawing.

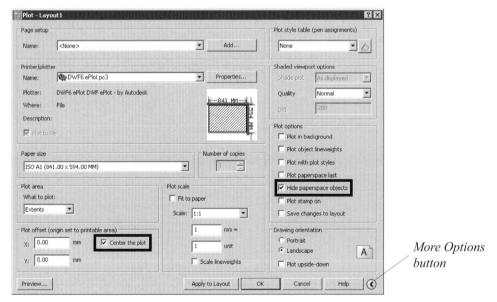

Figure 10.10. The Plot dialogue box fully expanded

*On large drawings you may want to plot part of the drawing. This used to mean twiddling your thumbs whilst waiting for the plot to complete before you could continue drawing. In AutoCAD 2005, placing a check in **Plot in background** allows you to immediately return to editing the drawing.*

Calculating the Sheet Size

One of the most confusing aspects of CAD is that drawings are drawn at full size on screen and the scale of the final drawing is decided after the drawing is complete, which is completely the opposite way to manual drafting, where the scale and sheet size are chosen at the outset.

When plotting time comes around, one of the most commonly asked questions is 'How do I calculate what drawing scale and sheet size I need?' Fortunately it is straightforward.

Assuming you are plotting from **Model Space**:

Take our MGM Electronics drawing as an example – it has limits set to 30000 units in the X direction and 25000 units in the Y direction. (In practice, however, I would not use the limits of the drawing, preferring to measure the distance to the extremities of what was actually drawn, with the **INQUIRY/Dist** command. This is because the limits of the drawing may be far too large, which would give you a false idea of the drawing extremities and result in a large expanse of white paper with a small drawing somewhere in the middle.)

Say you decide that the final plot scale should be 1:50. What sheet size will the drawing fit onto?

■ Divide the X direction (30000) by 50 and repeat for the Y direction.

This gives a plotted size of 600mm × 500mm. The plotted drawing will fit onto an A1 Standard Metric size sheet (841mm × 594mm) and there should be enough space around the drawing for your border and title information.

At scale 1:100 your drawing would fit onto an A3 sheet (420mm × 297mm) with a plotted size of 300mm × 250mm, but you must remember that the textual information may be too small to read!

Chapter 11 – Drawing Exercises

Introduction to Drawing with Coordinates

Drawing in AutoCAD can be done in many different combinations. We shall concentrate on 2D drawing with the use of **X** and **Y** coordinates.

In 2D, you specify points on the **XY** plane (also called the construction plane), which is similar to a flat sheet of grid paper. The **X** value specifies **horizontal distance**, and the **Y** value specifies **vertical distance**. The origin point **(0,0)** indicates where the two axes intersect.

In an AutoCAD drawing, the default origin point **(0,0)** is at the bottom left hand corner of the drawing, as shown in Figure 11.1.

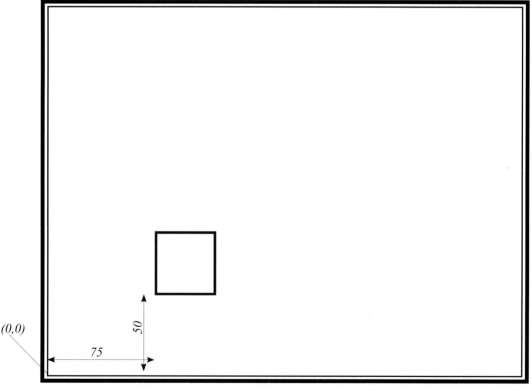

Figure 11.1 A representation of the AutoCAD drawing screen

138

Absolute Coordinates

Absolute coordinates are specified in an **X** and **Y** direction from the datum base point **(0,0)** and are always entered as (x,y) in that order. For example

75,50

would specify a distance of **75** units along the horizontal **X** axis and **50** units up the vertical **Y** axis to the specified point, as shown in Figure 11.1.

Relative Coordinates

Relative coordinates specify a position in the X and Y axis in relation to the current position. For example

@50,0

would move the cursor relative to the current position by **50** units in the **X** axis and **0** in the **Y** axis: a horizontal line. A vertical line would be entered as **@0,50**.

Polar Coordinates

Polar coordinates use a **distance** and an **angle** to locate a point. For example

@50<45

would specify a point 50 units from the previous point, at an angle of 45° relative to the previous point.

AutoCAD measures angles in an anticlockwise direction, as shown in Figure 11.2.

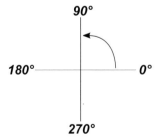

Figure 11.2 AutoCAD method of measuring angles

Exercise 1
Target Drawing

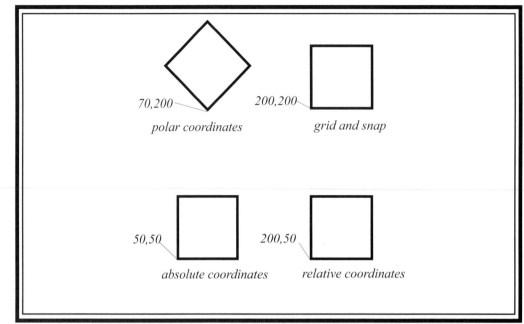

We will practise inputting coordinates by drawing four squares. The objective of this is to show you that using different methods achieves the same result.

The squares have sides of length 50 units. We will start with the bottom left hand square, completing it by using **absolute coordinates**. The bottom right square will be completed with **relative coordinates**, the top left with **polar coordinates** and the top right using the **grid and snap** feature, which does not rely on coordinates for input.

Drawing with Absolute Coordinates
■ Use **DRAW/Line**

Command: _line Specify first point:	**50,50**	**Enter**
Specify next point or [Undo]:	**100,50**	**Enter**
Specify next point or [Undo]:	**100,100**	**Enter**
Specify next point or [Close/Undo]:	**50,100**	**Enter**
Specify next point or [Close/Undo]:	**50,50**	**Enter**
Specify next point or [Close/Undo]:	**Enter**	

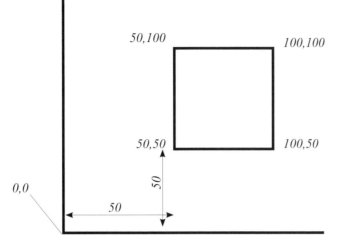

Figure 11.3 The first square, drawn with absolute coordinates

Drawing with Relative Coordinates

You will notice that, when drawing with relative coordinates, to travel in a negative **X** direction (to the left) or in a negative **Y** direction (downwards) the distance must be preceded with a minus (–) sign as can be seen below. You will see also that the first line is started with an **absolute** coordinate to locate the drawing in relation to the origin of the drawing **(0,0)** – the bottom left corner.

■   Use **DRAW/Line**

Command: _line Specify first point:	**200,50**	***Enter***
Specify next point or [Undo]:	**@50,0**	***Enter***
Specify next point or [Undo]:	**@0,50**	***Enter***
Specify next point or [Close/Undo]:	**@–50,0**	***Enter***
Specify next point or [Close/Undo]:	**@0,–50**	***Enter***
Specify next point or [Close/Undo]:	***Enter***	

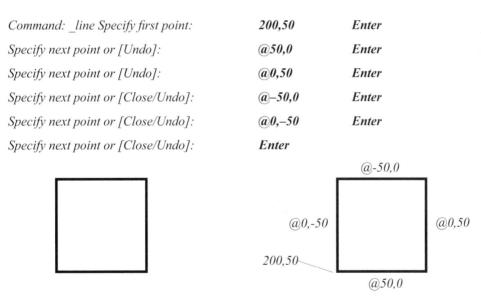

Figure 11.4 The bottom right hand square completed with relative coordinates

Drawing with Polar Coordinates

Remember that we are starting again with an absolute coordinate, and that 50 is the line length. Remember also that any figure following a '<' specifies an angle.

■ Use **DRAW/Line**

Command: _line Specify first point:	**70,200**	***Enter***
Specify next point or [Undo]:	**@50<45**	***Enter***
Specify next point or [Undo]:	**@50<135**	***Enter***
Specify next point or [Close/Undo]:	**@50<225**	***Enter***
Specify next point or [Close/Undo]:	**@50<315**	***Enter***
Specify next point or [Close/Undo]:	***Enter***	

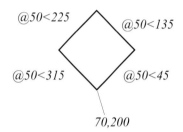

Figure 11.5 The top left square completed with polar coordinates

Drawing Accurately with Snap and Grid

You do not always have to use coordinates to draw accurately. As you work, you can turn **Snap** and **Grid** modes on and off, and you can change the snap and grid spacing.

Snap mode restricts the movement of the cross-hairs to intervals that you define. When **Snap** mode is on, the cursor seems to adhere, or 'snap', to an invisible grid. You can control snap precision by setting the X and Y spacing.

The grid is a pattern of dots that extends over the drawing area. Using the grid is similar to placing a sheet of grid paper under a drawing. The grid helps you align objects and visualize the distances between them. The grid will not appear on the plotted drawing. If you zoom in or out of your drawing, you may need to adjust grid spacing to be more appropriate for the new magnification.

Snap spacing does not have to match grid spacing. For example, you might set a wide grid spacing to be used as a reference but maintain a closer snap spacing for accuracy in specifying points.

■ To turn on **Snap** and **Grid** use **TOOLS/Drafting Settings** and the **Drafting Settings** dialogue box will appear, as shown in Figure 11.6.

■ Click on the **Snap and Grid** tab at the top of the dialogue box, as shown in Figure 11.6.

■ To turn on **Snap** and **Grid**, place ticks in the **Snap On** and **Grid On** checkboxes, as shown in Figure 11.6.

■ In the **Snap X Spacing** and **Grid X Spacing** boxes enter the number 10, as shown in Figure 11.6.

■ Click on **OK**.

You do not need to enter a value in the **Snap Y spacing** and the **Grid Y spacing** as they will adopt the values of the X settings automatically.

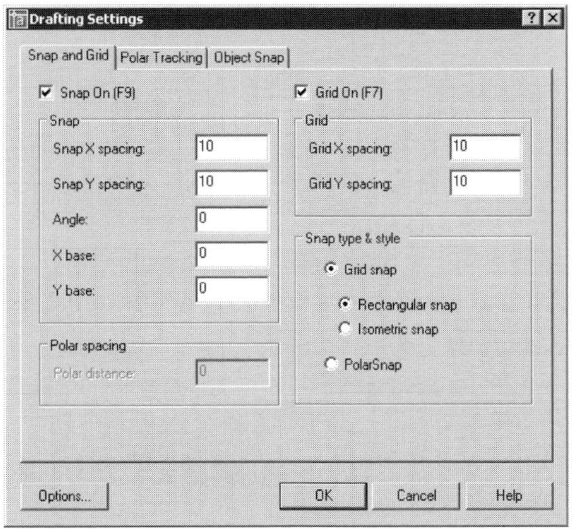

Figure 11.6 The Drafting Settings dialogue box with Grid and Snap values set to 10

■ The dialogue box will disappear and a grid of dots will appear on the screen, as shown in Figure 11.8. Move the cursor around the screen and you will see it 'jumping' or snapping to the grid intersections.

We are now ready to draw the fourth square.

■ Use **DRAW/Line.**

■ Move the cursor until the coordinate display in the bottom left corner registers **200,200**, as shown in Figure 11.8.

■ Click on the **Grid** point.

■ Using the coordinate display move the cursor to the other three corners, drawing lines to complete the square using the coordinate values shown in Figure 11.7.

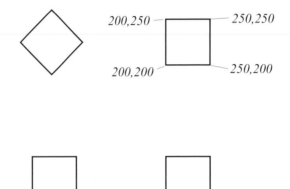

Figure 11.7 *The completed fourth square showing the absolute coordinate values*

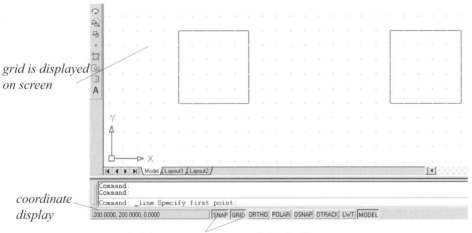

grid is displayed on screen

coordinate display

click here to turn Snap and Grid off

Figure 11.8 *The coordinate display showing the start position for the fourth square*

Exercise 2
Target Drawing

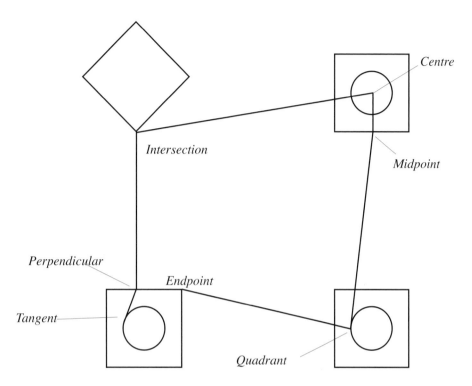

Make sure you have read the section 'Drawing with Object Snap' on page 43 before continuing.

Using **Object Snap** we will draw lines to specific points on the drawing.

SNAP ■ Turn **Snap** off.

■ Draw three circles of any size in the squares as shown in the Target Drawing.

■ Use **DRAW/Line** and start at the bottom left hand square with **Endpoint** as shown in Figure 11.9.

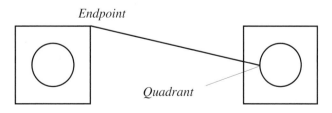

Figure 11.9 *The bottom squares with a Line drawn using Endpoint and Quadrant object snaps*

Command: _line Specify first point: **_endp of (Pick as shown in Figure 11.9)**

Specify next point or [Undo]:   **_qua of (Pick as shown in Figure 11.9)**

Specify next point or [Undo]:   **_mid of (Pick as shown in Figure 11.10)**

Specify next point or [Close/Undo]:   **_cen of (Pick as shown in Figure 11.10)**

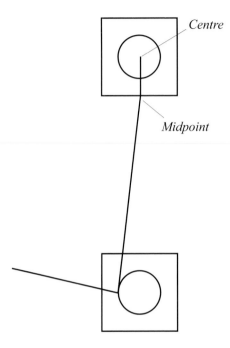

Centre

Midpoint

Figure 11.10 *The bottom and top right squares with a Line drawn using Midpoint and Centre object snaps*

Specify next point or [Close/Undo]:   **_int of (Pick as shown in Figure 11.11)**

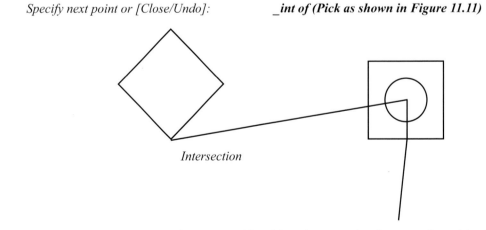

Intersection

Figure 11.11 *The top left square with a Line drawn using Intersection object snap*

146

Specify next point or [Close/Undo]:	**_per to (Pick as shown in Figure 11.12)**
Specify next point or [Close/Undo]:	**_tan to (Pick as shown in Figure 11.12)**
Specify next point or [Close/Undo]:	**Enter**

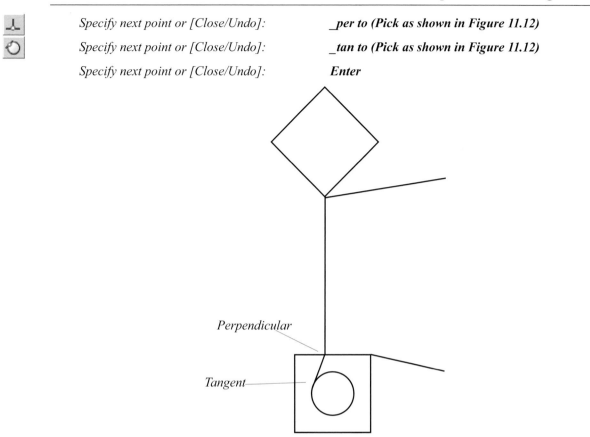

Figure 11.12. *The bottom left and top left squares with Lines drawn using Perpendicular and Tangent object snaps*

Exercise 3
Target Drawing

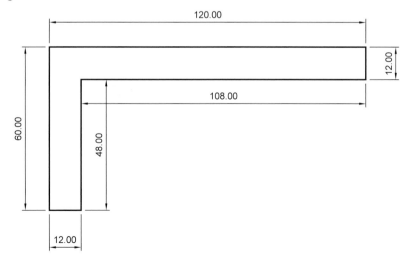

Exercise 4
Target Drawing

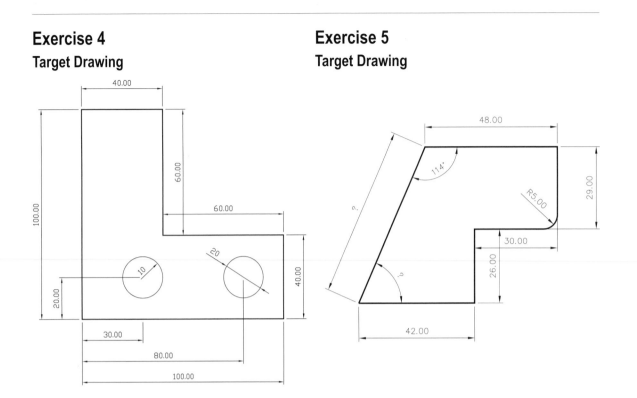

Exercise 5
Target Drawing

Exercise 6
Target Drawing

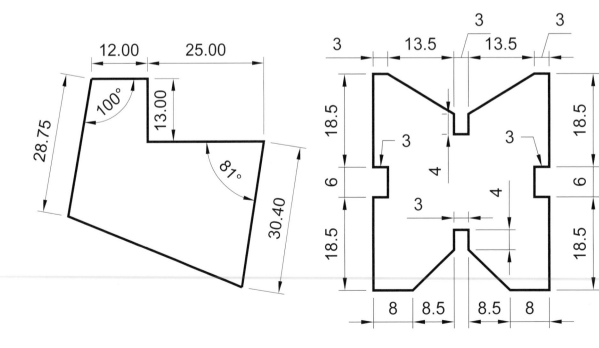

Exercise 7
Target Drawing

Exercise 8
Target Drawing

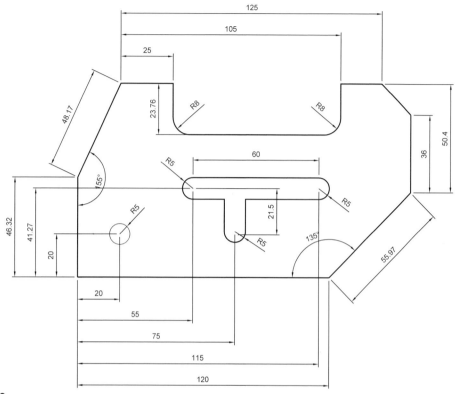

Exercise 9
Target Drawing

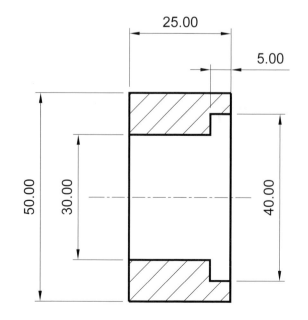

Index

Symbols

< 4, 9
@ 4, 8, 9
3D 114
3DFace command 119

A

Arc command
  Start, Centre, Angle 56
  Start, End, Direction 59
  Start, End, Radius 57
Area command 92
Arrays
  polar 67
  rectangular 38
Array command 38
AutoCAD
  activating 1
  closing 12
  earlier versions vi

B

Background colour 2
Blocks
  creating 60, 70
  exporting 60, 78
  inserting 71
  rules for drawing 60
Border
  inserting a pre-drawn 131
Break command 25, 30

C

Chprop command 115
Construction Line command 54
Continue Dimension command 100
Coordinates
  absolute 8, 139, 140
  introduction to 138
  polar 8, 139, 142
  relative 8, 139, 141
Copy command 75

D

Decimal units
  setting 13
Design Center 77
Digitising tablet
  overlay 6
  puck buttons 6
Dimension. *See also* Continue
  Dimension command
  angular 100
  baseline 99
  leader text 100
  linear 98
  Modify dialogue box 94
  Quick Leader 100
  Styles dialogue box 94
  Text Edit 100
  toolbar 98
Dimensioning
  and Annotating 94
Dimension Style
  setting up 95
Door reveals
  adding 29
Drafting Settings
  dialogue box 15, 143
Drawing
  making look solid 116
  moving around 29
  the boundary wall 79
  the building 20
  the driveway 82
  the glazing 45
  the roof 117
  the windows 36
  with 3D coordinates 118
  with arcs 53
Drawing aids 14

E

Ellipse command 69
Enter 4, 21
Erase command 46
Esc 4
Explode command 75

Extend command 32

Extend command 32
  switching to Trim 39
External References 130

F

Function keys 4

G

Grid
  turning on/off 4
Grid and Snap
  drawing accurately with 142

H

Hatch
  dialogue box 90, 124
Hatch patterns
  creating 90
Help 4
Hide command 116

I

Inquiry toolbar 93
Isometric planes
  cycling through 4

K

Keyboard 4

L

Layers
  changing 36
  colours 17
  creating 16
  dialogue box 16
  drawing with 16
Linetype
  changing 83
Line command 55
List command 7

M

Menu

150

Other titles by Jeff Roberts:

Introduction to AutoCAD LT: A Companion Guide

Introduction to AutoCAD 2000

Introduction to AutoCAD 2000 (licensed) published by BPH, Calcutta, India.

Two-Dimensional CAD, City & Guilds 4351-01 Level 3 for AutoCAD 2000 Completed Examination Papers

Introduction to AutoCAD 2002

Introduction to AutoCAD 2002 (licensed translation) published by Soho Graph, Serbia.

Introduction to AutoCAD 2002 (licensed) published by Software Publications, Sydney, Australia.